Public Relations in the Military

Public Relations in the Military

The Scope, Dynamic, and Future of Military Communications

Bob "Pritch" Pritchard, Mari K. Eder,
Kim Marks Malone, Matthew Kroll,
Katie Cousins, Skye Martin

BEP

BUSINESS EXPERT PRESS

Leader in applied, concise business books

First published in 2022 by
Business Expert Press, LLC
222 East 46th Street, New York, NY 10017
www.businessexpertpress.com

ISBN-13: 978-1-63742-407-0 (paperback)
ISBN-13: 978-1-63742-408-7 (e-book)

Business Expert Press Public Relations Collection

First edition: 2022

10 9 8 7 6 5 4 3 2 1

Description

This book takes an in-depth look at the function of public relations as it exists in the U.S. military in the 21st century. There have been several books and journal articles covering the military/media relationship but none that delve into the breadth and depth of the responsibilities of today's military public affairs officer (PAOs). This book discusses the concept and foundations of military public affairs (relations), the changing strategic landscape in communications, operational planning and execution, and the people who practice military public affairs. As public relations is a function of command whose importance continues to increase, all military personnel, especially leaders, profit from a clear understanding of the benefits and limitations of public relations.

Keywords

military; public relations; public affairs; history; professionalism; ethics; strategic communication; information apocalypse; segmentation; internal information; external information; community relations; advising; public relations counsel; communication leadership; organizational leadership; education and training; qualifications; joint service

Contents

List of Table and Figures..ix

Testimonials xi

Preface xiii

Acknowledgments.. xvii

Part I	Concept and Foundations.. 1
Chapter 1	Introduction to Military Public Affairs 3
Chapter 2	History of Military Public Affairs (Relations)...................7
Chapter 3	Professionalism and Ethics..17

Part II	The Changing Strategic Landscape in Communications 25
Chapter 4	The Information Apocalypse..27
Chapter 5	The Fourth Estate 37
Chapter 6	The Road Ahead...45

Part III	Operational Planning and Execution......................... 53
Chapter 7	RPIE—Research, Planning, Implementation, and Evaluation...55
Chapter 8	Internal Information...63
Chapter 9	External Information 67
Chapter 10	Community Relations 79
Chapter 11	Breadth and Depth of Responsibilities.............................85

Part IV	The People Who Practice Military Public Affairs 89
Chapter 12	Who Are Military PAOs?..91
Chapter 13	Education and Training 99
Chapter 14	Public Affairs Specialty Qualification and Accession 107
Chapter 15	Public Affairs Employment..121

| Part V | The Future of Military Public Affairs .... 125 |
| Chapter 16 | The Way Forward ....127 |

Notes..145
References 153
About the Authors...167
Index 173

List of Table and Figures

Table 3.1   Basic DoD directives and instructions
             applicable to public affairs 20

Figure 4.1   The media bias chart...30
Figure 7.1   Michaelson and Macleod's best practices model..............56
Figure 7.2   Michaelson and Stack's B.A.S.I.C. communication
             objective measurement model..57
Figure 7.3   The Excellence Pyramid..61
Figure 14.1 The Chart to LCDR...112
Figure 14.2 The Chart to CDR 113
Figure 14.3 The Chart to CAPT...114
Figure 14.4 Air Force PAO Career Planning Diagram 117
Figure 14.5 CG Public Affairs Chain of Command.........................118
Figure 14.6 Structure of Typical CG Public Affairs Office 118
Figure 16.1 The Peso Model 136

Testimonials

"Public Relations in the Military *is a game changer, providing that rare combination of interesting, insightful and informative guidance for leaders and practitioners alike. This book should be mandatory reading for every serving military officer.*"—**Brig. Gen. Robert Hastings, APR, Fellow PRSA, Former Principal Deputy Asst Secretary of Defense, Public Affairs**

"*Right now, more than ever, forthright communication with the public about our military is fundamental to our democracy, and military public relations is critical to that mission. That is not the case in all nations; just ask a Russian citizen. As a Presidential Appointee in the last administration and as a General Officer, I always had the public's attention. Whether I was testifying to Congress or being interviewed by the media about the capabilities of the newest weapon system, my PAO was always at my side and saved my career on several occasions. As one star wing commander I had a public affairs debacle that got the CSAF attention. He sent me a personal note that simply said, "use your PAO." I still have that note.* Public Relations in the Military *is a must-read book for senior military officers and NCOs. I suggest that our service academies and Professional Military Education programs use this book in their curriculum. I wish I had the opportunity to read* Public Relations in the Military *20 years ago.*"—**The Honorable Robert F. Behler, Former Director of Test and Evaluation, Office of Secretary of Defense, Major General (ret), USAF**

"*The authors, all established military public affairs practitioners, have created an excellent resource for commanders, rising communication professionals and anyone who wants to better understand the critical importance of timely and accurate information flow in a democracy. Concise, comprehensive and elegantly written, this handbook is a must have for those who serve.*"—**Rear Admiral Stephen Pietropaoli, U. S. Navy (Ret.). Former Navy Chief of Information**

Preface

"There's no way I'm going to do anything more than the most basic aspects of public affairs. I don't want to get fired."

For decades, this was the common mantra of the military commander. Deeply rooted in the mid-grade officer's negative experience with the media during the Vietnam War, engaging in public affairs was seen as risky business. Media interviews were to be scrupulously avoided because one could get fired by saying something wrong or not in accord with guidance from above. Engaging with the community was not helpful either as there would always be detractors, complainers, and activists hostile to the command's mission.

Over time, the more enlightened commanders began to embrace public relations as a force multiplier and found greater success in achieving their mission through active rather than passive communication strategies. Public affairs has eventually been more fully embraced at all levels of command and many public affairs officers now have a permanent seat at the decision-making table.

Today, public affairs and the need to communicate strategically have never been more important. Global communication is instantaneous and state and nonstate actors have perfected mis-information and cyberattack capabilities. Fake news, the corruption of channels of communication, and the critical role of domestic and international support are required for military operations to be successful to round out the threats facing commanders today.

Public affairs, properly planned and executed, can blunt and defeat these threats. But just as the complexity of the operational environment has grown, so too has the communication environment gotten more complicated. As a result, it is more important than ever for commanders to have a more robust understanding of the public affairs function.

To aid in that understanding, this book takes an in-depth look at the function of public relations as it exists in the U.S. military in the 21st century. It discusses the concept and foundations of military public affairs, the changing strategic landscape in communications, operational strategic communications planning and execution, and the people who practice military public affairs. Our focus with regard to personnel is on the PAO as they are the leaders and managers of the command's public affairs efforts. Enlisted public affairs specialists are integral to those efforts as well and tend to be confined to executing tactics, except in the Coast Guard, where enlisted members carry more responsibility due to the small size of the specialty in that service.

Each of the authors of this text was handpicked to represent the Army, Navy, Marines, Air Force, and the Coast Guard. They are award-winning public relations specialists, both active duty and retired, with the full gambit of public affairs responsibilities at every level of command in the joint or combined environment.

Two of the authors are the members of the Public Relations Society of America's College of Fellows, the gold standard of public relations professionals. A rigorous peer review process has singled out these professionals as among the "best of the best." Candidates for the College of Fellows need to demonstrate superior professional performance and evidence of superior contributions to the field of public relations and having advanced the state of the profession. They also need to demonstrate significant service and leadership and that they have exhibited personal and professional qualities as a role model for others. Election to the College is considered the pinnacle of one's professional career.

Another two of the authors hold PRSA accreditation in public relations and military communication (APR+M). It signifies that the individual meets all the requirements of Accreditation in Public Relations (APR) and has demonstrated additional skills in military public affairs.[1]

The book is divided into five parts. The first part introduces the concepts and foundations of military public relations; the second part explores the changing strategic landscape in communications. Part III, operational planning and execution, includes a focus on the three major functional areas of internal information, external information, and community relations, as well as an overview of the breadth and depth of PAO responsibilities. Part IV delves into the people who practice military public affairs, including their education and training, service unique characteristics, and how one becomes a PAO. Finally, Part V looks at the future of the PAO.

The information environment is extremely complex and constantly changing. Decisions in the communication realm are among the most strategic and consequential a commander will make today. Fully understanding military public relations is the key to maximizing its potential in helping achieve mission objectives.

Acknowledgments

The authors would like to acknowledge and thank Don Stacks, Professor Emeritus, for his faith and confidence in this project. We would also like to thank our families and colleagues for their patience and support as we put this manuscript together. A special thanks to Stephen Pietropaoli, retired Navy Rear Admiral and former Navy Chief of Information, and Navy Lieutenant Commander Jacqueline Pau, USS Theodore Roosevelt PAO, for their insights and recommendations. Finally, we'd like to thank Lt. Col. Jean Duggan, United States Air Force and Maj. Kip Patterson, United States Army, both Defense Information School faculty members, for their help with the education section.

PART I

Concept and Foundations

Part I of this book defines the concepts and sets the foundation for the practice of public affairs (relations) in the U.S. military in the 21st century. Chapter 1 provides a broad overview of the profession as it is structured in today's military, including details of the fundamental roles and responsibilities of the public affairs officer (PAO). Chapter 2 offers an historical perspective of how the profession came into being in the U.S. military. The last chapter in this section covers foundational guidance and ethical and legal considerations for which every PAO, regardless of service, is accountable.

CHAPTER 1

Introduction to Military Public Affairs

In 2019, U.S. Strategic Command won a Silver Anvil, the Public Relations Society of American's prestigious award honoring outstanding strategic public relations programs. The awards have been given each year since 1944 "to organizations that have successfully addressed challenging issues with exemplary professional skill, creativity and resourcefulness."[1]

Their winning campaign was the result of direction given by General John E. Hyten, then Commander of U.S. Strategic Command, to the command "and in particular his PA [Public Affairs] team to aggressively pursue action to grow the public dialogue on 21st Century Strategic Deterrence."[2] General Hyten understood that public affairs was "the ambassador of facilitating informed perceptions about USSTRATCOM missions and objectives and communicating accurate, timely and meaningful information in context with the *Commander's Vision and Intent*."[3]

This is one example of many of the power of public affairs in achieving the commander's mission and intentions. In addition, Public Affairs offices play a key role in contingency and deployed operations.[4] The Army says it well:

> Public affairs fulfills the Army's obligation to keep the American people and the Army informed and helps to establish the conditions that lead to confidence in America's Army and its readiness to conduct operations in peacetime, conflict and war.[5]

The term "public affairs" is confusing to some. In the civilian world "the public affairs function of an organization aims to influence public policy, [and] build and maintain strong relationships with legislators."[6] The military uses the term to identify the formal command function devoted to communication, especially with the media and various other stakeholders. Public Affairs personnel are similar in many ways to their civilian sector public relations colleagues. They develop effective communications programs using the RPIE (Research, Planning, Implementation, and Evaluation) model used by their civilian counterparts, as exemplified in USSTRATCOM's winning Silver Anvil entry above. Public Affairs personnel have an extremely important *boundary spanning* responsibility, keeping the finger on the pulse of public opinion so they may provide counsel to senior leaders, while translating what the command is doing to external and internal stakeholders to achieve mission success. From the top leaders of the Department of Defense to the commanders of all manner of tactical units, Public Affairs continues to be recognized as key and essential personnel.

Public Affairs has its roots in the formal practice of what is now commonly referred to as "public relations," which dates to the early 20th century. The origins of the military's use of the term "Public Affairs" did not start becoming apparent until the late 1950s and early 1960s. Originally, each service used different terms to designate offices that were responsible for public communications and their titles ranged all over the map. The Marine Corps established a publicity bureau in 1907 in Chicago, Illinois. The Army created a Public Release Office, supervised by a then Maj. Douglas MacArthur, at West Point in 1916. And the Navy called their original 1917 Public Affairs office the Navy News Bureau. At the same time, the federal government created an all-encompassing, World War I communications team known as the Committee on Public Information (CPI). By the 1920s, the military branches, and most of the federal government, adopted the newly developed term of public relations as the official title for their communications offices and officers. After the end of World War II (WWII), the term "public relations" became too associated with "spin" and persuasive tactics, so the Navy and Coast Guard decided to use the term "public information" beginning in 1946. This is why the word "information" is so prevalent in the services today. The first public affairs school, the Army Information School, was established that same year and had later become the Defense Information School (DINFOS). Moreover, the Chief of Naval Information was first designated in 1950, a title that remains to this day.

In the post-WWII era, military public affairs programs mostly aimed to inform the public of upcoming and past military operations. As the civilian and academic fields of public relations progressed through the 1950s and 1960s, so too did the benefits of communication for military operations. This is one of the reasons many branches shifted to the term "Public Affairs" by the late 1960s and early 1970s. The updated term allowed for a broader application of external communications tactics, which would help commanders recognize public affairs as an operational asset.

John Kirby, a retired Navy Rear Admiral and twice former Assistant to the Secretary of Defense for Public Affairs, provided a comprehensive case for public affairs as an "operational" function in an essay written while he was at the Naval Command and Staff College. Among other insights, he pointed out that:

> … public affairs is relevant across the spectrum of conflict. It can be employed aggressively during peacetime to deter hostilities and during conflict to help leaders communicate intent and foster domestic support. During the post-hostilities phase of an operation, public affairs also demonstrates U.S. and allied commitments to peace and stability and aids in the restoration of law and order.[7]

The Public Relations Society of America today defines public relations as "… a strategic communication process that builds mutually beneficial relationships between organizations and their publics."[8]

Public Affairs shares many similarities with civilian public relations including researching, planning, budgeting, executing, and evaluating operations involving the public, liaising with news media, and providing guidance to senior leaders on decisions that impact mission success.[9] This includes (wording adjusted to align with the public affairs mission more closely):

- Staying alert to and interpreting public opinion, attitudes, and issues that might have an impact, for good or ill, on the operations and plans of the command.

- Counseling leadership at all levels of the command regarding policy decisions, courses of action, and communications—including crisis communications—considering their public ramifications and the command's social or citizenship responsibilities.
- Protecting the reputation of the command, the Services, and the Department of Defense.
- Continuously researching planning, implementing, and evaluating courses of action and communication strategies to achieve the informed public understanding necessary to the success of the command's mission.
- Managing the resources needed to do all this by aligning public affairs objectives with commander's intent, managing budgets, and developing staff.
- Overseeing the creation of content to drive stakeholder engagement and buy-in.[10]

Accession will be discussed more in-depth later in this manuscript, but officers typically enter public affairs after they have completed a four-year college degree and met service-specific qualifications. Enlisted public affairs personnel may enter the field directly upon enlistment or transfer from other specialties. Job training for both primarily consists of classroom instruction and on-the-job learning in various training environments. Like other members of the armed forces, they also complete a comprehensive training program covering responsibilities, military structure and etiquette, traditions, and leadership development.[11]

CHAPTER 2

History of Military Public Affairs (Relations)

It is not the aim of this chapter to provide the definitive history of military public affairs. It is, however, important to trace the evolution of the profession to understand how the field has grown far beyond media relations into today's force multiplier and an important management function.

That said, any discussion on military public relations must necessarily start with the military–media relationship. Since the founding of our nation and her armed forces, there has been tension between the public's right to know and the need to protect military information that might be useful to an opponent.

For the most part, military commanders have understood that providing information to the public is necessary to foster positive public opinion and support for the services' role in national defense, though it has not always been an easy sell. George Washington is said to have complained bitterly about both loyalist and patriotic newspapers during the Revolutionary War.[1] John Adams had newspaper editors publicly flogged.[2] Andrew Jackson jailed and attempted to court martial a newspaper editor during the New Orleans campaign.[3]

Prior to the Mexican American war in 1846, the press operated freely if their views corresponded to local views. Information gathering was haphazard and usually based on other publications, letters, and government proclamations. There were no reporters in the field. Military leaders were concerned, however, that some news undermined the war effort, though they were powerless to control it.

By 1846, technology and newsgathering had improved to the point where reporters were competing daily for news. The telegraph and the pony express offered speedy transmission of news and correspondents routinely deployed with the military. George W. Kendall, founder of the *New Orleans Picayune*, was known to report from the front lines and spent time with generals. Newspaper accounts were still up to 10 days old, despite efforts like Kendall's and the arrival of the telegraph. "Camp newspapers" came into being to keep the troops informed (a prototype for later military public affairs efforts). Civilian newspapers were known to use these "camp papers" as a primary source.[4]

Reporting on military conflict became quite problematic during the Civil War. The telegraph made it possible for the first time to report military action in real time. Government and military leaders, both North and South, did all they could to contain these reports. President Lincoln, though, saw the press as a means to maintaining popular support and so did all he could to keep the press unfettered.[5]

Lincoln is often credited as one of the first national leaders to recognize the need to have someone solely responsible for dealing with the media and ensuring the public was informed of the activities of the military. The person he put in charge, Charles A. Dana, managing editor of the *New York Tribune*, was appointed Assistant Secretary of War and oversaw handling the media and keeping the nation informed of Union military operations.[6] The foundation for military public affairs was laid.

The Spanish-American war was marked by two significant factors: substantial advances in technology and "yellow journalism." Printing presses were motorized, the trans-Atlantic cable had been laid, and telegraph lines ran the width and breadth of the Nation. And Joseph Pulitzer's *New York World* was locked in mortal combat with William Randolph Hearst's *New York Journal*. Some claim that the Spanish-American war was the result of machinations of the two enterprises engaged in simply to drum up sales and publicity for the two papers.[7] In any event, the atmosphere lent itself to severe government restrictions with the banning of reporters in combat zones and the closing of cable offices. None-the-less, information continued to be "leaked" to the public, making government retaliation largely ineffective.[8]

The most restrictive period in the military–media relationship was World War I. Initially, it was not so. The Committee on Public Information created by President Wilson upon America's entry into the war in April 1917, and headed by former newspaper editor George Creel, mounted an impressive program to mobilize public opinion in support of the war effort. More informally referred to as "The Creel Committee," this agency was governed by a set of regulations drawn up by the State, War, and Navy departments that placed restrictions on publication of militarily sensitive information like troop movements, sailing schedules, antiaircraft or harbor defenses, identification of units dispatched overseas, and the like. The press voluntarily abided by these regulations.[9]

But then Congress, prompted primarily by a national patriotic fervor that reached the level of wartime hysteria and concern over internal hostile and disloyal activities as well as the effects of propaganda, enacted the most onerous restrictions in history with passage of the Espionage Act in 1917 and the Sedition Act of 1918. The Espionage Act forbade publication of any information that might remotely be regarded as providing aid to the enemy. The Sedition Act prohibited any criticism of "the conduct or actions of the United States government or its military forces, including disparaging remarks about the flag, military uniforms, [and] similar badges or symbols ..."[10]

Reporters had to be credentialed as either accredited or visiting correspondents, swore an oath to write the truth, put up a $10,000 bond, and signed an agreement to submit all correspondence, except personal letters (which were censored elsewhere in the system), to the press officer or his assistant.[11]

The military–media relationship grew more robust in World War II. This was probably due to the nature of the conflict and the fact that patriotism was the order of the day. The Office of War Information and the Office of Censorship were created by President Roosevelt in 1941, the latter of which issued detailed guidelines on what could not be published. Included in the list of restrictions were location; identification and movement of units, ships, and aircraft; war production and supplies; weather forecasts and temperatures in major cities; casualties; and even locations of art treasures and archives.[12]

Accreditation was used by the military to control access to the battlefield. Correspondents got a press pass from the War Department and a passport from the State Department and once deployed, they were assigned to "press camps" that were attached to regular military forces. All administration, communication, and briefings were handled by the press camps. Typically, press camps consisted of some fifty correspondents, and each moved with a field army through Western Europe.[13]

Accredited correspondents wore officer's uniforms without rank insignia. Visitors, who could wear civilian garb but had to receive special permission to travel in the war zone, were accompanied by an escort officer and had to stick to a fixed itinerary. [14]

Most of the engagements in the Pacific theater of operations were maritime and Naval Chief of Operations Ernest J. King placed severe restrictions on military correspondents, frequently holding unfavorable reports until they could be paired with favorable ones. It was also far easier to control the media because correspondents were obliged to travel aboard U.S. Naval vessels and relied on the ship's communications equipment to transmit reports. Eventually, though, the Navy got better at the release of information, but only after journalists, editors, and publishers complained enough about the Navy's performance that the Office of War Information stepped in to force changes.[15]

General Douglas McArthur was even more restrictive with the correspondents traveling with him. He required multiple layers of censorship and frequently pressured reporters to change the tone of their stories to show the troops—and especially him—in a more favorable light.[16]

Initially in the Korean War, there were no restrictions on either media access to the war zone or on content. The media covering this "police action" adopted their own guidelines and voluntarily censored themselves. Predictably, this led to security leaks and confusion on the part of the media. Critics were quick to point out that the negative reporting by the media was eroding public opinion in the United States. But it was the Overseas Press Club that eventually petitioned the Defense Department to impose censorship so the media would know what its limits were.[17]

Thus, a system like that existing in World War II was instituted, with censors reviewing each story. The previous reports on inferior U.S. equipment, corruption in the South Korean government, or food shortages and panics were now forbidden. McArthur once again took things even further by disallowing stories that he (or his censors by proxy) considered would be harmful to morale or cause embarrassment to the United States, its allies, or the United Nations.[18]

In Vietnam, the media were free to move about the country, taking advantage of military transportation when it was available, and there was no censorship. Stories, photographs, and film were unimpeded by security review. For the media, this was the high-water mark in its relations with the military. Unfortunately, many military officers blamed the media for its "defeat" in that conflict, so Vietnam also gave us the low-water mark in that relationship.[19]

This opinion that the media lost the Vietnam War became deeply engrained in some of these officers and stayed with them as they rose through the ranks. The result was their ability to convince the Reagan Administration in 1983 to ban media access to operations in Grenada. The military was able to operate without regard to media scrutiny, which equated to success in the eyes of those senior commanders who distrusted the media. But criticism by the media was significant and vociferous, and rightly so. The good news is this tension drove both sides to find a better way to do things.

The initial response from the military was the creation of the Department of Defense (DOD) *Principles of Information*, which were issued on December 1, 1983.[20] In addition, Chairman of the Joint Chiefs of Staff John W. Vessey, Jr. appointed retired Major General Winant Sidle in 1984 to head a panel to study the issue. Vessey invited participation from the heads of major media organizations like the American Newspaper Publishers Association, the American Society of Newspaper Editors, the National Association of Broadcasters, and the Radio-Television News Directors Association.[21]

Their report, released in August 1984, contained eight recommendations that were intended to ensure news media coverage of U.S. military operations "to the maximum degree possible consistent with mission security and the safety of U.S. forces." One of the key recommendations of the "Sidle Report," as it became known, endorsed media pools in combat zone when other methods of providing access to the media were not feasible. A second notable recommendation was that access to military operations would be governed, as a basic tenant, by voluntary media compliance with security guidelines or ground rules established by the Defense Department. Violation of those guidelines or ground rules meant exclusion from further coverage of the operation.[22]

The first test of these new rules was the invasion of Panama in 1989. Unfortunately, the Pentagon's planning and response was poorly organized, much too slow and did not involve the local military commanders upon whose support the public affairs effort was dependent. As a result, the media were not able to cover that operation until the critical phases of the conflict were over.[23]

After a very critical self-evaluation, the Pentagon went back to the drawing board and under the able and energetic guidance of Assistant Secretary of Defense Pete Williams completely revamped its DoD National Media Pool procedures. Williams also got former Associated Press Pentagon reporter Fred Hoffman involved in analyzing the media aspects of Panama. Chairman of the Joint Chiefs of Staff Colin Powell also emphasized to his commanders the importance of including public affairs planners as part of the overall operations planning and this emphasis dramatically improved attitudes about the media within the military.[24]

Against that backdrop, both the Pentagon and the media worked hard for the six months prior to the liberation of Kuwait in 1991 (Operation Desert Storm) to organize the influx of nearly 1,600 journalists in the combat zone and keep them fed with information. The coverage of the Gulf War was the most comprehensive to date but was not without its difficulties. The media complained of their treatment, particularly with two aspects of the operation; the requirement that there be a public affairs escort with them wherever they went and the military's overreliance on media pooling. Once again, representatives of media organizations and the Pentagon worked together to develop the *DOD Principles for News Media Coverage of DoD Operations*, which was published in 1992. This simply reiterated what had previously been published but served to reinforce the importance of the military commander's personal involvement in planning for media coverage of future conflicts.[25]

During the operations in Haiti and Somalia, the lessons learned were successfully applied. The level of cooperation between the military and the media was robust, and planning for news coverage had the full attention of everyone in the planning process from the commander on down.[26]

The relationship continued to improve as the military services continued to find innovative ways to accommodate the media. *Operation Allied Force*, the NATO air war against Serbia that sought to put an end to the ethnic cleansing campaign being perpetrated against the ethnic Albanian population in Kosovo by the military and paramilitary forces of then-Yugoslavian President, Slobodan Milosevic, presented numerous physical and political challenges to media coverage of the conflict. The Navy and Marine Corps, which provided critical sea-based and expeditionary forces, proactively embarked news media in aircraft carriers and with Marine amphibious forces for coverage from the tip of the spear.[27]

While the air campaign was tailor-made for land-based air, the political environment made direct coverage of the employment of those forces difficult. To overcome these obstacles, the Air Force innovatively embarked correspondents in their B-52 bombers conducting combat missions.[28]

Yet there were still shortcomings to this inventiveness. Too few correspondents could take advantage of these opportunities, the media complained. The solution often advanced by the news organizations was free and unfettered coverage of the war zone.

In response, the Assistant Secretary of Defense for Public Affairs, Tori Clarke, and her staff prevailed on the Bush Administration, with the *support* of military commanders, to embed journalists with combat units, should it become necessary to act in Iraq. They would be able to report "real time" without censorship or security review. A handful of prohibitions had to be agreed to, all common sense, such as not providing specific locations and movements of troops, but reporters would be right in the thick of things, basically free and unfettered.[29]

Planning was intensive and more than 600 journalists completed the recommended one-week course to familiarize them with military operations and equipment—a kind of mini-boot camp. The media too began to do some planning of its own, which contrasted greatly with their response to preparations for the first Gulf War.[30]

The U.S. Navy played a crucial role in the opening military response to the 9/11 attacks, codenamed Operation Enduring Freedom (OEF). As Dr. Gregory Bereiter, Naval History and Heritage Command, notes in his summary, *The U.S. Navy In Operation Enduring Freedom, 2001–2002*:

> Attacks against al-Qaeda and Afghanistan's Taliban regime required a deep-strike capability in one of the most remote parts of southwest Asia where U.S. military forces initially had no access

to forward land bases. Because Afghanistan was landlocked and positioned nearly 400 miles from the nearest sea at its southernmost border, carrier-based strike aircraft and ship-launched cruise missiles played a foremost role in the campaign. This was the first time that the U.S. military prosecuted a war from aircraft carriers, TLAM–armed vessels, and land bases positioned so far away from the combat zone.[31]

In anticipation of combat operations and to deal with these challenges, the Navy preemptively embarked 30-40 journalists in naval strike force assets, including aircraft carriers and Tomahawk shooters.[32]

Soon, embed preparations paid dividends. When the first troops crossed the line of departure into Iraq, on their way to Baghdad, correspondents went with them. Some of the most enduring images of those first hours and days were of reporters like David Bloom reporting live from HUMVEEs as they rolled through the Iraqi desert. Reporters were getting shot at along with their units. It was not just American journalists who crossed over with the troops. Reporters from around the world traveled with them. Even *Al-Jazeera* had embedded correspondents. *Washington Post* columnist Howard Kurtz called it "old-fashioned war reporting, but with razzle-dazzle technology that brings it into our living rooms in real time."[33]

The War on Terror, which arguably began during the attacks on September 11, 2001, that were broadcast on live television to millions of viewers around the world, sparked the current era of the military–media relationship. Coupled with the immense growth of online, independent, and cable news outlets, the media's need for information is unlike any previous time in history. To complicate this relationship even more, the credibility of many outlets is difficult to determine and the trust of media is quickly decreasing. This is leading some military commanders to an opinion of the media like that of the Vietnam Era.

Throughout the military's history of Public Affairs, the title of this function changed to match its operational intent. From "Publicity" and "Public Relations" in the 1920s and 1930s to "Public Information" in the post-WWII era, and then to "Public Affairs" after Vietnam, we can see the proverbial pendulum swing from one side to the other. To show the current realization that the media are a positive tool for operations, we simply need to look at the adoption of the emerging term "Strategic Communications" that is quickly finding its way into military policy.

For the most part, military commanders have understood that providing information to the public is necessary to foster positive public opinion and support for the services' role in national defense. We are at a pivotal point in history, where the military–media relationship can flourish or flounder. Will military commanders learn from the lessons of the past, or will the pendulum continue to swing?

CHAPTER 3

Professionalism and Ethics

Just as with every other occupational designation in the military, public affairs has its own set of standards, qualifications, and expectations. Part IV of this text goes into some depth on the education and training of Public Affairs Officers (PAOs), the process of and qualifications for accession, and service unique characteristics. While the details of these may differ slightly by service, they are all basically in alignment. This chapter covers foundational guidance and ethical and legal considerations for which every PAO, regardless of service, is accountable.

The primary philosophy/guidance under which every PAO operates is the *DOD Principles of Information* contained in DoD Directive 5122.05.[1] It sets the standard for all DoD Public Affairs activities and "applies to the full continuum of day-to-day activities and operations. It is the commander's responsibility to ensure that all planning for military activities and operations efficiently and effectively achieve the goals set by these principles."[2]

The full text of Section 5.1 of DoD Directive 5122.05 is provided here for ease of reference.

> 5.1 It is the policy of the Department of Defense to make available timely and accurate information so that the public, Congress, and the news media may assess and understand the facts about national security and defense strategy. Requests for information from organizations and private citizens will be answered in a timely manner. In carrying out the policy, the following principles of information will apply:
>
> (a) Information will be made fully and readily available, consistent with the statutory requirements, unless its release is precluded by current and valid security classification. The provisions of Section 552 of Title 5, USC, also known as the "Freedom of Information Act," will be supported in both letter and spirit.

(b) A free flow of general and military information will be made available, without censorship or propaganda, to the Service members and their dependents.

(c) Information will not be classified or otherwise withheld to protect the U.S. Government from criticism or embarrassment.

(d) Information will be withheld only when disclosure would adversely affect national security, threaten the safety or privacy of Service members, or if otherwise authorized by statute or regulation.

(e) The DoD's obligation to provide the public with information on its major programs may require detailed public affairs planning and coordination within the DoD and with other government agencies. The sole purpose of such activity is to expedite the flow of information to the public; propaganda has no place in DoD public affairs programs.[3]

These five fundamentals complement the DoD Principles of Information and describe best practices to follow when fighting in the global information battlespace.

1. **Tell the Truth**. Military PA personnel will release only truthful information.

2. **Provide Timely Information**. Commanders should be prepared to release timely, coordinated, and approved information about military operations.

3. **Practice Security at the Source**. All DoD personnel are responsible for safeguarding sensitive information. As sources of information, each DoD member should be aware of operations security (OPSEC) issues, whether being interviewed by the media or sharing information with family or friends.

4. **Provide Consistent Information at All Levels**. Commanders should ensure that DoD PA operations put forth a consistent message through its many voices. Information should be appropriately coordinated and in compliance with official DoD and supported command guidance before it is released to the public.

5. **Tell the DoD Story**. Every military and civilian member of DoD should help provide accurate information about the armed forces and national defense operations to the public. Commanders should educate and encourage their military and civilian employees to tell the DoD story by providing them with timely information that is appropriate for public release.[4]

In addition, DoD Instruction 5400.14 implements policy, assigns responsibilities, and prescribes procedures for the conduct of public affairs programs in support of joint, combined, and unilateral military operations.[5] Together, these policies provide the foundation for the conduct of each service's specific regulations on public affairs.

Beyond this foundational guidance, DoD directives and instructions address several issues specific to the conduct of public affairs. Table 3.1 provides the basic DoD Directives and Instructions applicable to public affairs.[6] For a full listing of directives and instructions impacting public affairs, please see the Accreditation in Public Relations + Military Communication (APR+M) Study Guide.[7]

DoD Directive 5500.7 and DoD Instruction 5500.7-R provide all military members with a broad ethical framework, though neither is specifically focused on public affairs. DoD Directive 5500.7 specifically addresses ethics in section 4.3., which states that "DoD personnel shall perform their official duties lawfully and comply with the highest ethical standards."[8]

DoD Instruction 5500-R focuses on gifts, use of Federal government resources, gambling, outside employment, and activity and use of military title by retirees and reserves. The instruction also covers travel benefits, conflicts of interest, political activities, financial and employment disclosure, and postgovernment service employment.[9]

While these directives and instructions provide foundational guidance for all members of the military services, public relations professionals face ethical challenges unique to the profession and far different from any other branch or specialty. As numerous scholars have noted, moral dilemmas are deeply embedded in public relations practice. White and Dozier note that as a boundary-spanning function,[10] public relations are regularly confronted with conflicting interests as part of their primary task

Table 3.1 Basic DoD directives and instructions applicable to public affairs

Directive	Title	Effective Date
DoD Directive 1000.11	Support and Services for Eligible Organizations and Activities Outside the Department of Defense	April 12, 2004
DoD Instruction 1000.15	Procedures and Support for Nonfederal Entities Authorized to Operate on DoD Installations	October 24, 2008
DoD Instruction 1300.15	Military Funeral Support	April 9, 2021
DoD Instruction 1300.18	Department of Defense (DoD) Personnel Casualty Matters, Policies, and Procedures	August 14, 2009
DoD Directive 2000.15	Support for Special Events	November 21, 1994
DoD Directive 2311.01E	DoD Law of War Program	May 9, 2006
DoD Instruction 5025.01	DoD Issuances Program	August 1, 2016, as amended
DoD Instruction 5040.02	Visual Information (VI)	July 8, 2016
DoD Instruction 5040.07	Visual Information (VI) Production Procedures	April 14, 2013
DoD Directive 5100.01	Functions of the Department of Defense and Its Major Components	December 21, 2010
DoD Directive 5105.74	Defense Media Activity	December 18, 2007
DoD Instruction 5120.20	Armed Forces Radio and Television Service (AFRTS)	October 18, 2010
DoD Instruction 5122.08	Use of DoD Transportation Assets for Public Affairs Purposes	December 17, 2014
DoD Directive 5122.11	Stars and Stripes (S&S) Newspapers and Business Operations	September 3,1996
DoD Instruction 5200.01	DoD Information Security Program and Protection of Sensitive Compartmented Information (SCI)	April 21, 2016
DoD Directive 5230.09	Clearance of DoD Information for Public Release	August 22, 2008, as amended

Document	Title	Date
DoD Directive 5230.29	Security and Policy Review of DoD Information for Public Release	April 24, 2017
DoD Directive 5400.07	DoD Freedom of Information Act (FOIA) Program	January 2, 2008
DoD Directive 5400.11	DoD Privacy Program	October 29, 2014
DoD Directive 5400.13	Joint Public Affairs Operations	October 15, 2008
DoD Directive 5400.14	Procedures for Joint Public Affairs Operations	November 3, 2014
DoD Instruction 5405.3	Development of Proposed Public Affairs Guidance (PPAG)	April 5,1991
DoD Directive 5410.15	DoD PA Assistance to Non-Government, Non-Entertainment Oriented Print and Electronic Media	March 28, 1989
DoD Instruction 5410.16	DoD Assistance to Non-Government, Entertainment-Oriented Media	July 31, 2015
DoD Instruction 5410.18	Public Affairs Community Relations Policy	November 20, 2001
DoD Instruction 5410.19	Public Affairs Community Relations Policy Implementation	November 13, 2001
DoD Instruction 5410.20	PA Relations with Business and Nongovernmental Organizations Representing Business	September 29, 2016
DoD Directive 5500.7	Standards of Conduct	November 29, 2007
DoD Instruction 5500.7-R	Joint Ethics Regulation	August 30, 1993
DoD Instruction 8550.01	DoD Internet Services and Internet-Based Capabilities	September 11, 2012
DoD Instruction 8910.01	Information Collection and Reporting	May 19, 2014
Secretary of Defense Memorandum	Installation Access and Support Services for Nonprofit Nonfederal Entities	December 23, 2014
Deputy Secretary of Defense Memorandum	Ensuring Quality of Information Disseminated to the Public by the Department of Defense	February 10, 2003
Secretary of Defense Memorandum	Interaction with the media	July 2, 2010
Joint Publication 1-02	Department of Defense Dictionary of Military and Associated Terms	March 25, 2014

Source: Public Domain, Department of Defense.

to create understanding between organizational and stakeholder expectations.[11] Neill and Drumwright[12] reported that public relations professionals they interviewed provided ethics counsel on issues that extended far beyond communication and traditional public relations responsibilities to include general management and strategic issues—issues of financial transparency, faulty product design, security breaches, and human resource issues related to inappropriate sexual conduct.[13]

To deal with these ethical dilemmas, military public affairs personnel can turn to the various service's core values. For the Army, these would be *Loyalty, Duty, Respect, Selfless Service, Honor, Integrity,* and *Personal Courage*. Navy and Marine Corps core values are *Honor, Courage*, and *Commitment*. The Air Force enumerates *Integrity First, Service Before Self*, and *Excellence in All We Do* as their core values. Finally, the Coast Guard lists *Honor, Respect*, and *Devotion to Duty* as its core values.

Military Public Affairs personnel can also rely on the Public Relations Society of America's *Code of Ethics*. There are three parts to the current PRSA *Code of Ethics*:

1. A preamble that sets out the goals and role of the document.
2. A statement of professional values, which identifies and describes six values of the public relations profession.
3. A list of six "codes provisions of conduct," each of which is elaborated with a core principle and examples of the provision in practice.[14]

The six professional values are:

- *Advocacy*—We serve the public interest by acting as responsible advocates for those we represent. We provide a voice in the marketplace of ideas, facts, and viewpoints to aid informed public debate.
- *Honesty*—We adhere to the highest standards of accuracy and truth in advancing the interests of those we represent and in communicating with the public.
- *Expertise*—We acquire and responsibly use specialized knowledge and experience. We advance the profession through continued professional development, research, and education.

We build mutual understanding, credibility, and relationships among a wide array of institutions and audiences.

- *Independence*—We provide objective counsel to those we represent. We are accountable for our actions.
- *Loyalty*—We are faithful to those we represent, while honoring our obligation to serve the public interest.
- *Fairness*—We deal fairly with clients, employers, competitors, peers, vendors, the media, and the public. We respect all opinions and support the right of free expression.[15]

The PRSA Code "Provisions of Conduct" are:

- *Free Flow of Information*—Protecting and advancing the free flow of accurate and truthful information is essential to serving the public interest and contributing to informed decision-making in a democratic society.
- *Competition*—Promoting healthy and fair competition among professionals preserves an ethical climate while fostering a robust business environment.
- *Disclosure of Information*—Open communication fosters informed decision-making in a democratic society.
- *Safeguarding Confidences*—Client trust requires appropriate protection of confidential and private information.
- *Conflicts of Interest*—Avoiding real, potential, or perceived conflicts of interest builds the trust of clients, employers, and the publics.
- *Enhancing the Profession*—Public relations professionals work constantly to strengthen the public's trust in the profession.[16]

In 2009, DoD took further steps to professionalize the public affairs field. Robert T. Hastings, principal Deputy Assistant Secretary of Defense for Public Affairs, signed a memorandum of understanding (MOU) with the Universal Accreditation Board for public relations professionals in February of that year. That MOU governed creation of "a professional development and Accreditation program geared toward personnel responsible for public affairs within the Department of Defense."[17]

The APR+M designation signifies an advanced public affairs professional who meets all the qualification of Accreditation in Public Relations (APR) plus additional requirements specific to military public affairs, including an emphasis on joint operations. Candidates for APR+M must first apply to ensure eligibility. Once eligible, candidates will complete a presentation to a panel comprising three APR+M accredited members. The panel presentation includes a questionnaire and portfolio review of public affairs work so panel members may assess competence in several areas not easily judged on the computer-based exam. The panel then makes a recommendation for the candidate to advance to the computer-based examination.[18]

There are 11 topics covered in the APR+M process. The ethics and law section covers everything from the Law of Armed Conflict to the Freedom of Information Act of 2016.[19] As APR+M candidates must also satisfy the requirements for APR, they are also tested on ethical integrity and behavior, First Amendment issues and privacy, and other legal issues.[20]

While each of the services has embraced APR+M in a slightly different manner, the credential improves the military public affairs profession, as do a host of additional credentialing opportunities. The commander who has these credentialed personnel on their public affairs staff can rest easy as they have the best military public affairs professionals possible.

Summary and Discussion

In this part, we provided a summary of the critical strategic communications roles and responsibilities of the PAO. We also looked back at the history of public affairs and the influence the military–media relationship has had on the evolution of the profession. Finally, we looked at the foundational guidance and ethical and legal considerations for which every PAO, regardless of service, is accountable. In the next part, we will look at the changing strategic communications landscape and its impact on military public affairs.

PART II

The Changing Strategic Landscape in Communications

In Part II, we examine the "Information Apocalypse" and the dangers presented by the confluence of more and newer technologies on trust. We also explore the precipitous decline in trust in the "Fourth Estate"—the professional media—and drill down into some of the factors that contribute to this decline. Included is some advice on how the PAO can navigate these shoal waters. Finally, we investigate our opportunities for managing the pace of change in today's communications environment, including our response to these changes, and how information is protected and revealed.

CHAPTER 4

The Information Apocalypse

We are careening towards a future where the ability to distort reality shakes the foundations of democracy

—Aviv Ovayda via Twitter[1]

No, there are no zombies. But there are bots and trolls, hackers, hijacked accounts, propaganda, and pretenders of all sorts. Lies and liars abound. How do military leaders and public affairs officers succeed in this toxic information environment and maintain the bond of trust with their communities, not to mention the people and organizations who support them? How can national security leaders continue to work with allies, recognize enemies, and respect ground truth? How do we engage a weary public on critical national security issues?

This is the real danger that people become numbed by the daily dose of news disguised as outrage, disappointed, and disgusted to the point they simply give up, stop challenging the multitude of falsehoods that confront them, and disengage from public discourse entirely. How can we reach them? What can be done, at the seat of government or by other institutions? What can we do as senior leaders? It comes down to the ways and means of telling truth and preserving trust, even as the apocalypse threatens to drown out all civility and destroy productive public discourse.

The Gallup management consulting company annually publishes the results of its poll on the most trusted institutions in the country.[2] With a 1–2 percent dip since 2019, the military nonetheless retains its high standing.[3] While the trust in newspapers and broadcast media has fallen in recent years, other American institutions have fared even worse. In 2016, Internet news, a new category, was rated low, probably due to abuse of privacy and manipulation of content, resulting in that figure continuing to drop. By 2021, the news media was clearly the most distrusted institution in the world.[4]

This absence of focus coincides with a substantial rise in propaganda.[5] Since its demise in the lexicon following World War II,[6] propaganda was confined for decades to political advertising and was easily recognizable. In the past 20 years, propaganda slyly insinuated itself into the mainstream, promoting points of view and causes with limited information of a factual nature. Propaganda became associated with celebrities and how they built their brand image and padded their resumes as well as their reputations.

There is a defined American cultural tendency to place public figures on a pedestal and revere them for their accomplishments. But the list of those who have been toppled from those pedestals since the 1990s is a long one, packed with prominent names, from almost every institution, including the clergy (thank the Catholic Church abuse scandals),[7] sports (e.g., doping of Russian Olympic athletes,[8] the Houston Astros trashcan banging[9] to announce pitcher's signs to their hitters, and professional football's deflate-gate controversy),[10] and political scandals (including those of governors like Schwarzenegger,[11] Spitzer,[12] and the forced resignation of Secretary of Labor Alex Acosta when his plea deal[13] with sex offender Jeffrey Epstein when he was a federal prosecutor in southern Florida was revealed to the public). Scandals from the world of entertainment are nearly too numerous to mention. But one name is more than worthy of mention. Harvey Weinstein's sexual assaults and rapes, his abuse of power[14] over many years in Hollywood, served to launch the "MeToo" movement. Finally, the celebrity reporters and well-paid news anchors from the mainstream news media itself come crowding in.

As we have witnessed a souring of ethics in public life,[15] we have become inured to our loss of confidence in those reporting news. Print and broadcast journalists have become major celebrities, with fans and followings of their own. Eventually, many fall from grace, including the likes of Brian Williams,[16] Charlie Rose,[17] and Matt Lauer,[18] victims of their own arrogance and false sense of invincibility.

Even entertainment world celebrities with their long history of non-conformist lifestyles have failed to titillate with their affairs and excesses in recent years. The debasement of language in movies, television, and song seems to have reached rock bottom itself, until the next shocking revelation. Yet we are unable to look away. Celebrities now influence more than personal choices in attire and cosmetics; they influence issues and even markets. In February 2018, Snapchat shares fell six percent in response to a tweet by celebrity influencer Kylie Jenner[19] who said, "Soooo does anyone else not open Snapchat anymore?"

The result of the toxic mix of American culture and apparent lack of standards is an appalling slurry of political excess, celebrity overindulgence, and hubris. To some extent, this negative atmosphere existed prior to today's polarized political environment. This polarization ushered in the beginning of a coarse new era and a significant drop in social norms, inviting disquieting lows in civil discourse, the standards for public service, and promoting excesses in personal behavior.

Unfortunately, our military leaders have not been absent from this stage. Sensationalized stories about the very public fall of former Generals David Petraeus,[20] Michael Flynn,[21] and Stanley McCrystal[22] come immediately to mind. The bottom line is that the very public failures of public figures erode our faith in the institutions they represent. We need our leaders, while not perfect, to live up to the standards they spent their careers espousing. We cannot be expected to believe their propaganda. And Public Affairs Officers cannot ignore or suppress coverage of these important stories.

Can we believe much of the news we see and read? Or perhaps, if one accepts that there are potential issues with factual reporting in all news coverage, the larger question becomes then why is the media not regulated by government? Why are there no ratings informing the public about veracity or reputation for impartiality?

Many restaurants in the United States post their sanitation ratings, yet when we read a political piece on a social media site there is no warning that it is not true, verified, or even reasonable. How do we know what we are getting? This is a singularly important question since most consumers have the inherent tendency to seek out news that confirms beliefs they already hold.[23] According to Irqa Noor,[24] a neuroscience and linguistics student at Harvard University, this factor affects not only news consumption but the search for confirmation of religious beliefs, politics, and human resource concepts. Even the well-traveled Media Bias Chart[25]

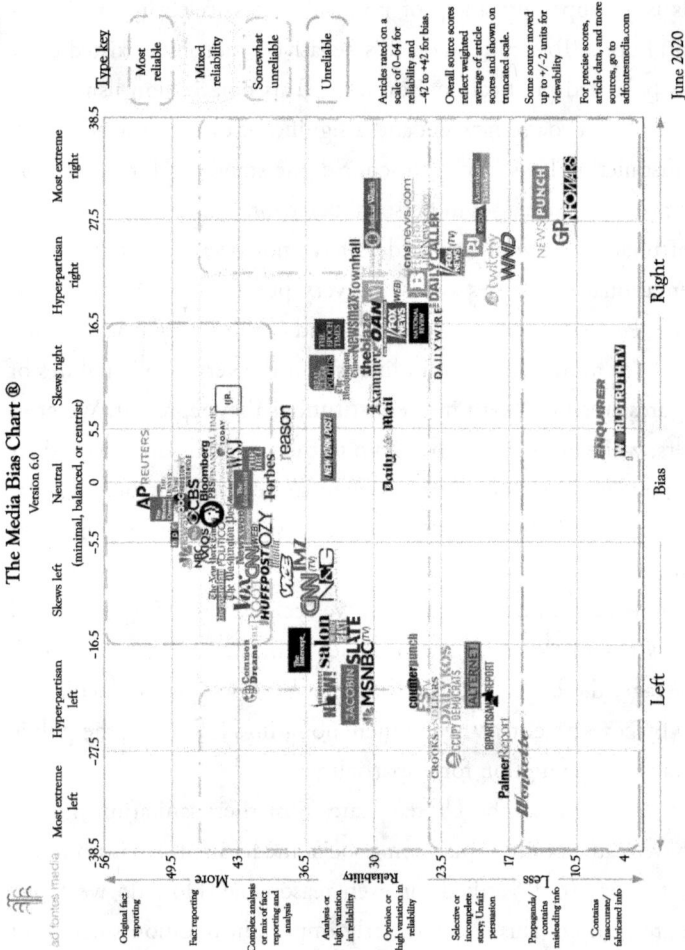

Figure 4.1 The media bias chart

(Figure 4.1) by Vanessa Otero that purports to assess various media by its focus is subject to interpretation; many may disagree with a medium's rating of news sources as liberal, conservative, or ultimately, unreliable.

While dangerous before, viral growth of the Information Apocalypse continues to grow at a pace matching that of the COVID-19 pandemic.[26] The issue of Russian interference in the 2016 and 2020 presidential elections has alarmed members of both parties and magnified the issue of social media responsibility.[27] The result is undeniable. Following the conclusion of the 2018 U.S./Baltic Summit, then National Security Advisor, then Lt. Gen. H.R. McMaster said, "Russia brazenly and implausibly denies its actions, and we have failed to impose sufficient costs. The Kremlin's confidence has grown, as its agents conduct their sustained campaigns to undermine our confidence in ourselves and in one another."[28]

More than 2.5 billion people (monthly users) access Facebook worldwide.[29] This global phenomenon has flattened distance and engaged and networked people across the world in ways never seen before. As a media platform, it is eclipsed in the United States only by YouTube which is used as a source of news and entertainment by 73 percent of all adults (and 94 percent of Millennials).[30] So with the explosive news that Cambridge Analytica had obtained data on 87 million users through a third party developer and that data were used in an attempt to influence voters in the presidential election, Facebook was forced to acknowledge its responsibility for protecting consumer data and its obvious failure to do so.[31]

Naturally, the question about regulation surfaces again and again, in the political theater that constitutes a public Congressional hearing. Should American lawmakers focus on regulating tech companies or permit them to continue to regulate themselves? Facing lawmaker's questions, Facebook's CEO, Mark Zuckerberg promised a number of changes to how Facebook is managed in an effort to increase security, authorizing ads, and protecting privacy.[32]

It is a different story in the European Union. There the General Data Protection Regulation (GDPR), which took effect in May 2018, is maturing in its efforts to better protect privacy through strictly regulating Big Tech data collection and enforcing consent.[33] It has already begun to fine companies.[34] California's data protection law was passed the same year. Other states are considering drafting their own legislation. At some point, the U.S. Congress may follow suit with an American version of such a law, but it is likely not to be a swift or easy change.

The *Edelman Trust Barometer* series delves deeply into the issues of institutional trust, going beyond that of information manipulation by foreign governments, trolls, political operatives, or false flag organizations to the more primal fear that information can be used as a tool of warfare itself.[35]

Global statistics on trust are fairly static but by 2018, the *Trust Barometer* revealed a staggering 37 percent drop in trust in all institutions in the United States. According to it, nearly 60 percent of adults say "I am not sure what is true and what is not," while over 56 percent say, "I do not know which politicians to trust," and 42 percent say, "I do not know which businesses to trust."[36] In 2017, a widely shared fake news story was that former President Barack Obama had signed an executive order banning schoolchildren from reciting the pledge of allegiance.[37] The story was read more than two million times. During the 2016 election cycle, fake news was circulated nearly 40 million times. The Russia-Trump collusion narrative of 2016 is probably the best known and most damaging of these fake storylines.[38]

Perhaps even more worrisome is the portion of the Edelman trust study that reveals rising global concerns regarding fake news as a weapon.[39]

In 2020, just a few months since the beginning of the pandemic, more than 16 countries passed new laws making the distribution of fake news about COVID-19 a crime.[40] Many countries had no need for new laws. There were already laws about the spread of false information on the books. China and India are two of the nations with the most stringent laws. Fake news has also disrupted elections in South Africa. In Singapore, the government is considering new laws to combat fake news while Germany now fines media companies for failing to delete fake news.[41]

In the United States, trust issues are broader than that of influence or manipulation but extend to actual distortion. Artificial intelligence (AI)[42] is a major factor in this area, from the long-criticized alteration of news photographs and digital video editing to computer-enhanced or even wholly created images, often not designated as such. Associated issues include AI used for decision making in a military context to direct drones, satellites, or other weaponry, all when a certain set of criteria are met and in conditions devoid of human oversight.

China is investing heavily in developing AI and its related technologies.[43] While AI has obvious business applications, it can also be used in military operations. For example, future computers could direct swarms of bots or order satellites to attack other satellites and destroy them. Once programmed with a set of parameters for decision making, it can be difficult to override those requirements. The danger here is the speed of application. Could warfare speed up to the point that people are unable to keep up with the decision-making process? Or that they are no longer even part of that process? We have a preview of that possibility from our front row seats here at the beginning of this change, as we watch the evolution of the driverless car and its decision-making capabilities cause accidents during trials. Not to mention its mistakes.

Just as the manufacturers of driverless cars must work hard to build consumer confidence, other businesses must continue to strive to protect privacy and build prosperity. Edelman states that employees typically trust their employers to do the right thing, with a global confidence level of 72 percent. Government and nongovernment organizations (NGOs) have further to go in restoring trust.[44]

In the latest in Gallup's tracking of the public's confidence in key U.S. institutions, trust in the Fourth Estate fell to 36 percent.[45] To fulfill its self-described missions to educate, inform, and entertain, the broad institution of media must do more to guard information quality, discipline itself, and protect the privacy of consumers.

According to a recent Pew Research Center study,[46] nearly 6-in-10 Americans (58 percent) say that they prefer to protect the public's freedom to access and publish information online, including on social media, even if it means false information can also be published. This means that individuals who reject regulation must do a better job of recognizing false information.

How can we challenge the lies? Public Affairs Officers should:

- Ask questions. Ask for evidence.
- Check the source. Is the URL for the story legitimate? For example, abcnews.com and whitehouse.gov are legitimate sites. Abcnews.com.co and whitehouse.org are not.
- Quotes by a general officer or other military or government leader can also be fact-checked and traced back to an event or statement.

- Photographs can be examined by reverse searching the URL on Google.

As producers of information and official positions or commentary, business and government leaders should aim for consistency and transparency in communication. They should perform as role models of professionalism and always act in accordance with stated organizational values. As such, PAOs must:

- Respond early to lies, outrageous charges, or fake news. Even if a commander does not have all the correct information or the right answers, it is more important to be able to say, "We are going to find out. We will investigate and will tell you what we learn."
- Know when to preempt potential negative news. There are times when internal briefings to family members—telling them first about a potential deployment, or an extension— can go a long way toward maintaining the bond of trust.
- Conduct background sessions with local media that explain processes and procedures. "This is how casualty notifications work. Here is how the process for a court martial unfolds. This is why we can trust vaccines."
- As for fake news or misinformation, call it out. No drama, no accusations, simply state the facts.

There are numerous sites that bill themselves as fact-checkers or scam debunkers but many are ineffective.[47] But awareness is the most important step and the one that should result in false information being exposed.

According to the American University, there are currently 10 reliable facts and bias-checking websites that are effective at examining news stories.[48] Now an emerging startup industry, more companies, and nonprofit organizations are coming online all the time. Hopefully continuing innovation coupled with media scrutiny can give service members the confidence to assess facts and recognize false narratives in news coverage.

Over the past several years, the Information Apocalypse has continued to grow. Upon reflection, perhaps this phenomenon might be better defined as a chaotic beginning to a new information age. It remains to be seen whether news, media, and Big Tech companies will take a positive role in correcting the pillars of their institution or whether the Fourth Estate will suffer from self-immolation only to rise from the ashes as a new being. Whether these changes will be for the good is something that all leaders can and should influence. That requires vigilance and sustained engagement.

The very nature of this continuing war on reason and common sense affects everything in the information domain, from command information to media relations and outreach. The PAO must work with cyber experts, diplomacy experts, and use the insights that strategic communications planning can offer to create ongoing tactical advantages in providing timely and accurate information to all audiences.

CHAPTER 5

The Fourth Estate

It is twice as hard to crush a half-truth as a whole lie.
—Austin O'Malley, Keystones of Thought[1]

The Fourth Estate is in a state of turmoil that has reached critical mass. Part of this state of affairs is the result of changing perceptions. The news media continues to be viewed as the single most mistrusted institution in the world.[2] This presents an entire series of problems to the PAO, who must deal with the media as a means of informing the public and internal audiences.

But now the primary problem facing by the media has descended to a lower level. There is a broad lack of public trust in media as a profession.[3] To take that one step further, there is considerable debate whether journalism even *is* a profession.[4] The common frameworks of professions and professionalism legitimize this question. In an essay on "The System of Professions," Dr. Andrew Abbott discussed the evolution of a number of professions such as medicine and law. He termed journalism as more of a "permeable profession" characterized by frequent movement between journalism and public relations with considerable influence exercised by each side of that coin on the other.[5]

In the United States, journalism is not regulated or credentialed. There are no annual training requirements, no *enforceable* ethical standards (you may be reprimanded, but there is no way to suspend or stop someone from the practice), and there is no body of accepted practice similar to those of the legal bar or medical associations. There is no single code of ethics, instead a mishmash of associations with their own codes. Abbot noted that there is also no exclusion of those who lack journalism education, training, or adherence to any recognized code of ethics.[6] While journalism may be composed of people with the job to report/edit/write the news and to do so with a sense of morality beyond that required by law or even society, this alone is not sufficient to meet the standards of a profession. Instead, what we loosely refer to as *the media* is a wide spectrum of individuals with varying capabilities, audiences, standards, and agendas. Has the quality of journalism suffered from this lack of professionalism, infused as it may be with public relations agendas, talking points, and ideas? This omission has also limited the development of journalism as a vocation, perhaps making it less appealing as a career choice.

A further blurring of lines between objective reporting and influence is the degree to which the Internet has democratized the media. One could have made a stronger case for media professionalism back in the early days of print and broadcast media when the number of outlets was limited, and the perceptions of quality were far higher. Advertisers helped fuel these perceptions by providing dollars only to sources they viewed as particularly trustworthy or "professional." But this has changed due to the Internet. Society's expectations of the media include information quality, educating people on important issues, and helping inform good life decisions.[7] Even Mark Zuckerberg insisted for a time that Facebook was a platform, not a publisher.[8] Yet, the American public has come to include social media in the category of "media." With social media being particularly vulnerable to fake news, this is a problem. Advertisers are pulling dollars away from the traditional print and broadcast outlets to seek greater returns of investment (ROI) online. In turn, traditional outlets are trying to stay relevant.

That has been a losing battle. The news media today is vastly different than it was even two years ago. Newspapers have been declining in readership in the past 20 years, with weekday circulation dropping from 60 million in 1994 to 35 million in 2018.[9] While local papers have had the most layoffs and greatest drops in circulation, the increase in digital news access has affected urban papers as well. Advertising is also in sharp decline. In September 2019, the *Washington Post* abruptly ceased distribution of its free *Express* paper.[10] The paper had an estimated readership of 240,000. Twenty staff members were laid off. As we drive deeper into the 2020s, one can envision a future without newspapers. Will local news sites fill the void?

That may be logistically impossible. Local newspapers are in even deeper trouble. If communities continue to call for action "defunding the police"[11] and simultaneously lose any semblance of local news coverage, then who is held accountable in government, business, or any other institution that is the bulwark of a functioning society? The result would be the ultimate death of not only trust but truth.

What of television news then? Can it step into the void? In general, television news is stagnant and, at least at the local and regional level, adhering to format and substance unchanged for decades. There is no discernable difference between local television news programs in 1989 and 2019; a half-hour block with five or six stories, top story leads, with the last five minutes covering sports and weather. Substance changes have been driven by cost. It is cheaper to rely on interviews than to actually cover events. And a recent Pew study showed that news stories were growing shorter while sports and weather began to expand.[12] What little substance there is can be further diluted by mandatory banter among the anchors. This is not news. It is old-fashioned entertainment, where the anchors appear trustworthy and believable—and it is losing out to Internet news.

It is true the local target demographic is typically older and less interested in using the Web as a resource. Yet, the rise of cable and the advent of the 24-hour news cycle have changed the national news coverage. But the same stories tend to repeat and the moniker of "breaking news" is much like the cry "Wolf!" Often there is nothing new of note.[13]

The notion of trust has been at the very epicenter of the Information Apocalypse. Here, "Trust" is measured a bit differently as the likeability and believability of individual journalists and new anchors come into play. One could argue that if the news media is becoming less trustworthy, it could be because the older television news model is better at building trust. A recent study showed Americans trusted news that they could rely upon to be accurate, have the latest details, used valued experts as sources, and provided information on sources as well as backup data.[14]

Information Sources Influence Trust

We are witnessing a collision between two conflicting sources of information.[15] On the one hand are the commercial sources that depend on the standard filter of traditional media and journalists. On the other hand are the Internet sources that are operating on a tenuous presumption that the Internet has flattened the world to the point that we can directly access ground truth and reality. Obviously, the Internet writ large has gifted us numerous conspiracy theories and ideas based on a false premise or faulty science. For example, think about the movement to prevent childhood inoculations for diseases like measles[16] or the fear generated in numerous communities by fraudulent science narratives that tied inoculations to autism.[17]

As consumers of news and information, we need a mechanism by which to judge whether or not there is a slant, agenda, or politics in the content being put out. Is an outlet decidedly right wing or left? Are we getting ground truth? People tend to seek out information that confirms what they already hold to be true. Amplified by algorithms that analyze our choices, Internet platforms oblige accordingly with the information brought to you because "You liked this before." Psychologists call this as "confirmation bias,"[18] the tendency to seek out information that confirms or supports beliefs already held.

Somewhere in between these news sources are an emerging model creating space for itself, where crowdsourced and funded outlets appear to have the beginnings of a workable formula for building an audience and securing financial support. The approachability and the format itself, which can appear as decidedly antiestablishment journalism to some, are apparently appealing to many.

The Young Turks (TYT), a subscription news service on YouTube (and a paid app), is now the largest online progressive news and talk channel in the world, with 4.56 million subscribers.[19] It features a number of additional outlets in its network, with top-rated shows featuring news, sports, politics, and talk for the connected generation. Its reporters and anchors likewise appear unlike typical journalists.

Potential viewers are warned—these popular programs are aimed at "the 98% of people not in power."[20] How does this channel pay for itself? A number of online fundraising campaigns have been highly successful, in direct contrast to the declining advertising model for the traditional media.

The rise of new journalism models like TYT is leading the shift. Even Facebook, which long resisted hiring reporters and paying publishers, announced a new Facebook News Tab in October 2019.[21] In an interview Mark Zuckerberg said, "We get that the internet has been very disruptive to the news industry … This is an important moment in our relationship with the news industry and with journalism."[22] We need to "do a better job of supporting journalism," he added.[23] The News page was launched in New York and plans are for it to become more widely available over the next year; its homepage will be managed by journalists, apart from editorial intervention by the company.[24]

Twin Crises

The media's twin crises of relevance and professionalism require both introspection and action. The first step is to come to grips with what purpose the profession serves—traditionally its role has been to inform, to educate, and to entertain. And because the profession serves society as a whole, access to media (access to the professional service) is a paramount concern. If indeed there is an audience that relies on traditional media because it is trusted more than social media, it becomes a professional matter to assure that access. It may be a bridge too far to regulate this unwieldy, widely varied field that we call journalism or news reporting. Perhaps it would be more logical to define or divide by type and focus.

Certainly, we do not expect the same level of professionalism from gossip columnists or sports reporters as we do from defense reporters who cover the Pentagon, State Department, or the White House. But the dumbing down of journalism has led us to be better judges of what many of today's reporters are actually undertaking. The focus is often not on telling a story but generating clicks and hits, which have become journalism's current coin of the realm.

To Improve Trust

Obviously, there is more that media writ large can do from within to build trust and gain back its once-believing audience. The biggest effort journalism can undertake in serious news coverage is to show transparency. *Who* was interviewed for a particular story? *What* are other sources? Journalists should eschew anonymous sources. Truth can no longer be taken at face value. Proof must be offered and willingly if insights are to be accepted. Broadcast journalists should disdain celebrity stories as news, resist cynicism and attitude in reporting, and stop repeating unfounded and salacious claims. Self-discipline in a profession notorious for its lack thereof can go a long way to rebuilding trust.

Journalists and editors alike can do a number of things to improve public trust in their work. They can easily increase transparency about their process for reporting and researching news.[25] When serving as the subject of an interview, senior leaders should know they have a right to information about the structure of a story so that they can understand the reporter's focus, agenda, and how the reporter, as someone outside government, is attempting to make sense of what is happening within. For example, a recent *Washington Post* Fact Checker story on false and misleading video ended with the comment, "Our work on this project was funded by a grant from Google News Initiative/YouTube. Readers can find the full description of the categories with additional examples at *The Washington Post's* manipulated video fact-checker site."[26]

Media literacy is paramount. While many schools in the United States have developed programs to teach media literacy, there is no national data on how the programs are working.[27] Aside from these programs, many adults have no idea where to begin to achieve this literacy. Senior leaders in particular need a sophisticated understanding of media processes and products. They need to be able to define what constitutes "fake" news, know how to recognize "sponsored" content, and understand how social media platforms attempt to influence subscribers and the public at large.

At all levels, consumers need to understand how the Information Apocalypse, driven by political and cultural agendas, accelerated by the Internet's global voices has changed and continues to change communication standards. Leaders must be determined to resist how the media time and space constraints tend to "dumb down" complex issues and multifaceted topics.[28] Fight for context and detail, insist on transparency, and continue to seek out engagement with media and with audiences of all kinds.

Nieman Labs journalism predictions draw on insights from a number of journalists. According to Colleen Shelby, a reporter with the *Los Angeles Times*, "We've been taught not to be the story, or divert from our priorities to inform the public and protect the truth. But if we want to continue to reestablish trust with our audiences and re-enforce our industry, now's the time to teach."[29]

And what is the PAO's role in this changing landscape? It is consistent with the values of the Profession of Arms: *to seek facts and speak truth*. It is the only way to build trust and confidence in military command information and in operational reports. This means ongoing work to continue to create and enforce ground rules, educate about, and get commanders ready to deal with media, to correct mistakes, and demand retractions when needed. In other words, the PAO cannot step back or withdraw from this fractured media–military relationship but has an increased responsibility for helping make it work.

CHAPTER 6

The Road Ahead

Great leaders have a vision of the future that does not yet exist, and an ability to communicate that vision. When we put words to the world we imagine, we can inspire others to join us in creating a brighter future.

—Simon Sinek[1]

The future is replete with opportunities for managing the pace of change, our response to change, and how information is protected and revealed. Governments are getting tougher on tech companies and are now exerting more influence to prevent the growth of monopolies in information sources. We can expect to see an increasing focus on antitrust legislation for media and tech corporations and a greater emphasis on the uses of artificial intelligence (AI) to detect disinformation and manipulated content, enforcing protections of both information and privacy of individuals.

Education and Insights

There is a critical need for increased education in assessing information for truthfulness and a greater focus on individual as well as corporate responsibility in the information domain. With the decline of civics classes in public schools, fewer and fewer students understand how government works. By 2016, only 23 percent of eighth graders performed at or above the proficiency level on a national-level civics exam.[2]

Of necessity, education is going beyond schools. Tech companies should help users to determine the truthfulness of available information, avoid hackers, and be able to recognize sites and scams with ill intent, all without violating individual rights either to offer opinion or purpose.

Numerous police departments now provide guides for parents on which social media sites may be inappropriate for their children.[3]

In the same vein, the FBI has developed educational programs for middle-school students that teach children how to be safe on the Internet. The FBI Safe Online Surfing (FBI-SOS) program is a nationwide initiative designed to educate children in grades three through eight about the dangers they face on the Internet and to help prevent crimes against children. It promotes cyber citizenship among students by engaging them in a fun, age appropriate, competitive online program where they learn how to use the Internet safely and responsibly. The program emphasizes the importance of cyber safety topics such as password security, smart surfing habits, and the safeguarding of personal information.[4]

These are just initial efforts to stem the tide of declining civics education in the United States. More needs to be taught, particularly in terms of how to make sense of news and public information. As Joshua Yaffa stated in a recent *New Yorker* article, "If you don't know how government actually works, you're more likely to believe in conspiratorial versions of its doings."[5]

Universities are quickly pursing their own paths to educating students about democratic processes, information streams, and their potential for manipulation. The University of Washington's 2018 online elective "Calling Bullshit" received an overwhelming response from students and educators.[6] The viral clamoring for more knowledge on how to counter misinformation led to the establishment of the *Center for an Informed Public*. Launched in December 2019, the Center's mission statement is to "resist strategic misinformation, promote an informed society, and strengthen democratic discourse."[7] The Center supports interdisciplinary research, courses, and publications on a broad spectrum of communications issues, ranging from misinformation regarding the COVID-19 pandemic to the role of bots and trolls in a crisis. Center professor, Dr. Carl Bergstrom commented on the Center's COVID communications research, saying, "This is a crisis unfolding in slow motion, in a statistical way where we can only see pieces of it." He says. "I recommend people pick one maybe two times a day to read what's going on from reputable sources like *The New York Times* or STAT or WIRED—and if you must go on Twitter, block the hashtags."[8]

Maintaining Engagement

Public engagement with media has remained strong, growing 22 percent in 2019, according to Edelman.[9] Social activism is likewise increasing. More individuals are involved in grassroots movements from #MeToo to #NeverAgain while Greta Thunberg, the Swedish teenager, making a point of how important environmentalism is to the future of the planet has her own book *No One is too Small to Make a Difference*.[10] Corporate involvement is rising. Amazon, Google, and Target are engaging in addressing the issue of climate change. A myriad of companies have addressed their sexual assault policies and inherent racism in hiring. As regards the issue of immigration, Apple CEO Tim Cook urged the U.S. Supreme Court to save the Deferred Action for Childhood Arrivals (DACA) program protecting hundreds of thousands of young immigrants from deportation.[11] In June 2020, when the Court ruled against the Trump administration's efforts to end the program, Cook said, "The 478 Dreamers at Apple are members of our collective family. With creativity and passion, they've made us a stronger, more innovative American company. We're glad for today's decision and will keep fighting until DACA's protections are permanent."[12]

Black Lives Matter[13] surged to front of mind for all Americans in the summer of 2020, the season of our discontent. The nonchalant murder of George Floyd on a city street in Minneapolis broke open a seeping wound of national shame and sparked a major outcry against the police, white supremacy, and the full, ugly history of institutional racism across the country. Confederate statues were toppled from their bases, the Confederate flag was finally folded, and America began to confront her troubling past and the issues spawned by institutional racism. At last, it seemed that this was the moment real change was possible.

But the spread of the coronavirus also impacted public awareness of racial inequities. According to an Edelman special report published in May 2020, "the spread of COVID-19 highlights the depths of racial disparity across the U.S."[14]

A Gallup poll conducted in June 2021 revealed that American's view on race relations continue to decline:

"… an increasing percentage of U.S. adults believe racism against Black people is widespread in the United States. Relatedly,

Americans' satisfaction with the treatment of Black people remains near its historical low.

At the same time, more Americans than a year ago believe civil rights for Black people in the U.S. have improved in their lifetimes … . A majority of Americans believe Black people are treated less fairly by police in their community than White people are, but most do not believe Black people are treated less fairly in other situations."[15]

Focused on Change

Other changes in public confidence in institutions have taken center stage as revealed by its 2020 Edelman Trust poll. This remarkable shift in confidence in institutions is highlighted by the public's growing trust in government to provide information about the pandemic. According to Edelman, trust in government sources surged 11 percent, with the public relying on government for protection at a level of trust not seen since World War II. Respondents wanted the government to continue to provide economic relief (86 percent), to get the country back to normal (79 percent), to contain the spread of the virus (73 percent), and to keep the public informed (86 percent).[16]

There are also great expectations for business to partner with government in improving the economy and building new job opportunities. This represents an inflection point for both business and nongovernmental organizations (NGOs). Never has the need been greater for collaborative and cooperative approaches to rebuilding not only the economy but also the underpinnings of society—education, access to health care, and opportunities for fair housing, good jobs, and the potential for living a full life. While the 2020 Edelman study revealed the pandemic has turned many trust variables around, the need for fair and accurate media coverage continues. The pressures of pandemic response represent a monumental opportunity for traditional news media to regain public trust and confidence. Trust in traditional media grew seven points from January to May 2020 but there is still considerable work to be done.

The media has a major role to play in reporting on the necessity for change in society as well as promoting education and civic engagement.

In order to fulfill its self-described mission to educate, inform, and entertain, the broad institution of media must do more to guard information quality, call out false narratives, discipline itself, and protect the privacy of consumers. Media organizations must transform to serve the public, to educate, and inform, not merely entertain and titillate. Journalists and editors must refrain from glorifying celebrity and adhere to a set of professional standards heretofore neither broadly defined nor enforced. Social media is also displaying increased signs of corporate responsibility. As of November 2019, Facebook more than tripled its employees working on security and safety. More than 35,000 digital media experts are now focused on AI, content review, machine learning, and more.[17]

As the public has become increasingly engaged with news, people are unwilling to merely accept information as it is delivered. Many now question sources, demand transparency, and explore references and sources. One would expect this to bode well for journalism; greater public cynicism should mean more thorough fact checking and increased awareness of scams, falsehoods, and hacks. There are more sites available today that support determining truth in news, both in terms of ferreting out manipulated media, from photographs to videos, and in determining false sources, lies, and bias.

As fallout from the pandemic continues to push democratic institutions to move beyond the Information Apocalypse, a number of efforts will become more prevalent and visible:

- Increasing focus on regulation of tech firms, antitrust cases, and a major focus on corporate responsibility for safeguarding privacy and truth.
- New respect for the planet, environment issues, awareness of the effects of global warming, and the creative abilities of science.
- Increased government and business efforts to protect privacy, stop hackers, find, and force out bots and trolls, delete false accounts, and call out those who incite violence.
- Growing transparency in intelligence and awareness that shared information can effectively prevent false narratives and influence campaigns.

- New applications for AI and the growth of facial recognition software application.
- Continuing discussion in the diplomatic arena of how war in cyberspace can result in war in the physical domains. The second- and third-order effects concerning cyber rules of engagement and legal rulings regarding justification for declarations of war will dominate military discussions.

These actions represent the signs of a coming transformation, a culture shift from the Information Age's "apocalyptic Wild West" to tomorrow's Knowledge Age. In this next generation of information, *trust will be paramount*. The responsibility for creating this massive cultural change lies with everyone: governments, business, NGOs, and the media—in short, with all institutions that have a stake in preserving trust and truth—and with all citizens. Thankfully, a harsh and dystopian future is not guaranteed. We need to consciously develop media literacy standards in education at all levels, mandate responsible media, and build public trust and confidence in the knowledge that the false will be found out and eliminated.

These transformative actions are significant in and of themselves, but it is critical to go further. According to futurist Anne Lise Kjaer, "Things no longer change over a generation or a decade, but from year to year, even month to month, creating new arenas for disruptive ideas and innovation to emerge … . Inevitably, this leads us to reconsider the future and our place within it."[18] We must act in order to make sense of the rapid pace of change, today and tomorrow, developing not just a media literacy but futures literacy.

Many organizations are going even further, determined to meet future challenges head on. These companies are scheduling foresight sessions, hosted by futurist companies like the Institute for the Future. The Institute and like organizations train business and government organizations to identify disruptors, recognize trends, develop opportunities for change management, and scout out indications of emerging possibilities. Today's volatile operating environment has leaders realizing the key to prevailing in an uncertain future lies in the ability to not only identify potential change but to adapt in advance.

The PAO and Change

PAOs have a tremendous responsibility in this arena and a heightened sense of awareness concerning new trends and ongoing challenges is essential. Beyond that, the PAO must first acquire the commander's trust, then build collaborative relationships with the staff—in intelligence, cyber, and information operations and with diplomatic officials and organizations. But at the most basic level, *responsibility for this change begins with the individual.*

Service members must take measures to secure and protect their privacy online and in the public space. Education must become more robust and available at all levels, not just in schools. Leaders must *drive* change within their organizations and cultures. While many experts predict digital life in the future will improve, they also caution that people must be engaged in the process to effect this transformation.[19] Foresight increases agility and the ability to adapt and ensures that the fears many hold today are fully addressed. Basic rights and economic fairness must be considered and watched carefully.

With effort, tomorrow's social media platforms will be increasingly socially responsible and committed to protecting the privacy and rights of its users. Future citizens will undoubtedly be better informed because they can have trust and confidence in the knowledge they possess, know their privacy is secure, and can trust their institutions. The Knowledge Age is there to be created, shaped, and developed by today's armed forces, policy experts, and government leaders. Everyone must embrace these innovations and reforms, insist on basic rights, fairness, and demand factual information that we can all trust, rely upon, and use with the utmost confidence.

Summary and Discussion

In Chapter 4 of Part II, we examined what we call the "Information Apocalypse" and how it threatens to erode trust, drown out all civility, and destroy productive public discourse. We also discussed ways and means of telling the truth and preserving trust as a counter to this apocalypse. In Chapter 5, we explored the precipitous decline in the American public's trust in the Fourth Estate and drill down into some of the factors that contribute to this decline. Included is some advice on how the PAO can navigate these shoal waters. Finally, in Chapter 6, we investigated the road ahead, focusing on the need for more media literacy and how public affairs contributes to those efforts.

In the following part, we will go through the broad tactical areas for which the PAO and his or her staff are responsible and how these areas are managed.

PART III

Operational Planning and Execution

This part deals with the specifics of the operational planning process and execution. We explain the three major areas of communication for which the PAO and his or her staff are responsible, which are internal information, external information, and community relations. This includes an explanation of how the communications professionals research, plan, implement, and evaluate their efforts in each area. Finally, we focus on the breadth and depth of the PAO's responsibilities.

CHAPTER 7

RPIE—Research, Planning, Implementation, and Evaluation

Just as each element of a command has its particular planning process, so too does public affairs. Effective communication plans and campaigns need to be clear, concise, and cohesive in order to address problems and capitalize on opportunities. These strategic plans are used to help the organization achieve:

- A proactive change in attitudes/communication (etc.).
- An increase of awareness.
- Actually get something done.

Public affairs officers (PAO) use a four-step planning process to identify issues, prevent, and manage crises. This process is known by different acronyms: Research, Planning, Implementation & Evaluation (RPIE), Research, Action planning, Communication, and Evaluation (RACE), Research, Objectives, Programming, Evaluation & Stewardship (ROPES), and so on. Whichever acronym you choose to use, the four-step process includes research, planning, implementation, and evaluation.

Wherever a PAO is posted, this strategic planning process helps lift the public affairs function from a strictly tactical approach to issues to a strategic approach, which includes measurement and evaluation of strategic actions along the way and a communication after-action (or evaluation) in addition to the formal after-action process once the plan is completed.

As mentioned earlier, the elements the four-step process are Research, Planning, Implementation, and Evaluation. These elements are similar to the Joint Operation Planning and Execution System (JOPES) process but are focused on the communication process.

Michaelson and Macleod's best practices model illustrates the lifecycle of the planning process (please see Figure 7.1 below).

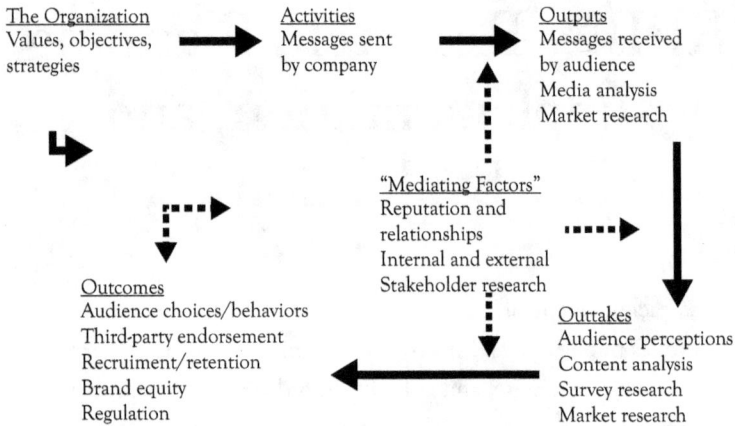

The Organization
Values, objectives,
strategies

Activities
Messages sent
by company

Outputs
Messages received
by audience
Media analysis
Market research

"Mediating Factors"
Reputation and
relationships
Internal and external
Stakeholder research

Outcomes
Audience choices/behaviors
Third-party endorsement
Recruiment/retention
Brand equity
Regulation

Outtakes
Audience perceptions
Content analysis
Survey research
Market research

Figure 7.1 Michaelson and Macleod's best practices model (used with permission)

Research provides the foundation for all the steps to follow. This stage starts with *developmental research*, which helps to identify whether the command is confronting a problem, challenge, or opportunity. A problem needs a solution, a challenge needs to be overcome, and an opportunity must be seized. Following developmental research is *secondary research*, or research that already exists. This information comes in the form of databases, articles, research reports, government and command documents, and the like.

Following the secondary research, the communications staff moves to *primary research*. Primary research is research that you conduct yourself and uses two basic methodologies: quantitative and qualitative. Quantitative research helps provide objective data obtained through specific research methodologies that can provide insights based on probability statistics. Qualitative research employs less manifest data and seeks a deeper understanding of information on attitudes and beliefs of specific personnel.

Once there is an understanding of the problem and the consequences of inaction, planning can begin. Just as in other military planning efforts, an analysis of the situation (or SA) is provided in the formal plan. This includes not only the research efforts but a stakeholder analysis (discussed in more depth later in this chapter), SWOT analysis, and competitive analysis.

From the insights garnered during research, a goal or goals are enumerated. Goals are single statements, rooted in the mission statement of the command, that reflect reputation management, relationship management, or task management. It is unnecessary to have all three.

From the goal(s) statement(s) comes the development of *objectives*. Objectives must be clear and measurable and deal with intended outcomes rather than procedures or outputs. Three levels of objectives are necessary, matching up with the three levels of learning: *awareness* (informational), *attitude* (motivational), and *action* (behavioral).[1] Michaelson and Stacks introduced the B.A.S.I.C. model in 2010 as a way to evaluate these communications objectives over the lifetime of the communications effort (see Figure 7.2 below). It is important for the strategic communications planner to "take into account where on the lifecycle the audience is … ."[2] For example, if the target stakeholder is at awareness, planners will need to figure out how to get that stakeholder sequentially "around the horn," to advocacy.

- B.A.S.I.C. communication objectives for public relations efforts:
  - Build awareness
  - Advanced knowledge
  - Sustain relevance
  - Initiate action
  - Create advocacy

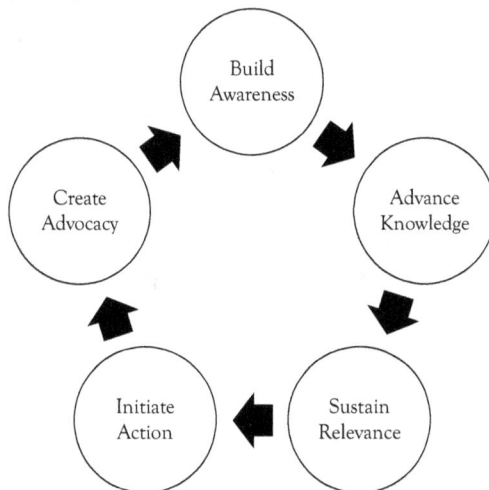

Figure 7.2 Michaelson and Stack's B.A.S.I.C. communication objective measurement model (used with permission)

With objectives in hand, the PAO and his or her staff can begin the development of communication strategies. These communication strategies are statements of communication themes or vehicles that will be used to accomplish a specific objective.

Tactics are next and are simply the actions needed to complete the strategy. A budget and timeline are then developed. Finally, a plan for measuring success during the campaign, as well as a plan for evaluating the campaign's effectiveness once it is complete, is put in place.

The implementation, or *execution* phase, is the process that turns strategies and plans into actions in order to accomplish strategic objectives and goals. In this phase, the focus of the communication staff is on managing stakeholders, managing content, and effectively carrying out and monitoring the plan.

The final phase in the communication planning process is *evaluation*. During this phase, the communications staff assesses the progress and results of the campaign or communication plan. Assessments are a tool to better align understanding of the information environment and to synchronize communication efforts. The data collected provide the ability to measure the effectiveness of the program against objectives. It also helps the communication staff to identify ways to improve and provides recommendations for the future. Planning for evaluation also helps the communications staff to adjust the plan, materials, and so on, before going forward and can serve as research for the next phase or program by providing examples of how to improve public affairs strategies and tactics and increase communication effectiveness.

One of the most important parts of the strategic planning process is *knowing your stakeholders*. Themes, messages, strategies, and tactics are determined by *who* the communication effort is trying to reach. The target audience consists of those people who are essential to achieving communication goals, so the PAO needs to understand who they are and what motivates them. Identifying the stakeholders and key publics within the target audience will enable PAOs to prioritize use of their communication resources, making them more effective and efficient.

Stakeholders are any group or individuals who are affected by or who can affect your command's successful achievement of the objectives. Stakeholders are required to participate for the communication plan or campaign to be effective. Examples of stakeholders include employees, military personnel, civilians in the local community, media, NGOs, and elected or government officials. Communication with stakeholders is based on the extent to which they may be affected by—or might affect—command operations or program outcomes.

A key public is a stakeholder that has become more active in their communication efforts. These individuals or groups have a shared interest in or concern about your command and their participation is required for the communication plan or campaign to be effective. Publics may emerge during a campaign, so it is important for Public Affairs Officers to continually assess the information environment. For example, adversaries or activists against the command may spread disinformation, misinformation, or mal-information. This will require that communication resources be prioritized to communicate with stakeholders and key publics about the disinformation, misinformation, or mal-information.

Both key publics and stakeholders have to be identified and combined into groups that best facilitate communicating with them. This is a process called *segmentation* and is the process of putting people or groups into subsets based on similar needs, values, and beliefs.

Characteristics used to segment publics and stakeholders include:

- Demographics: Who are they? (age, gender, marital status, income, education level, etc.)
- Psychographics: Why are they involved and with whom are they involved?
- Sociographics: What socioeconomic commonalities do they have?
- Motivating self-interest: What's in it for them?
- What is their relationship to the command and issue?
- Are they an influencer or intervenor within the community?
- What objective can they help you accomplish?
- What channels or platforms do they get their information from/on? How can you reach them with your messages?

Because time and resources are limited, it is also important for the communications staff to prioritize the need to communicate with the public based on the public's level of communication *activity*. Publics can be grouped into nonpublics, latent publics, aware publics, active publics, and intervening publics. Nonpublics are people who do not face a problem or opportunity and latent publics are people who could become active or aware of it but currently are not. Aware publics are people who recognize a problem and could become active. Active publics see that there is a problem or opportunity and are ready to act. An active public typically has a high level of involvement, think that their actions can affect the outcome, and are actively seeking information about the problem or opportunity. Intervening publics are the people who typically convey information to key publics and include media, opinion leaders, and third parties such as NGOs. Stakeholders and publics can also be grouped by attributes such as their importance to the command's success, whether they are a threat or an advocate, their power to influence, and their urgency or how quickly they might act.

The benefits of segmentation are numerous. It helps reduce clutter and increase clarity, helping make sure the communications staff has the most relevant and accurate information on key publics and stakeholders. Segmentation provides communication insights and improves stakeholder and key public engagement with the plan or campaign. Finally, all this helps make communication more effective and efficient.

What makes for an excellent communication plan? Scholarly research has suggested a model with three levels in the form of a pyramid (see Figure 7.3). At the most basic level, the campaign has done its research, stated its objectives, created its messages, targeted stakeholders, and evaluated the results. This is a successful campaign. At the intermediate level, the campaign has created deep connections with its stakeholders and publics, has been adopted by leadership, and sets new standards for creativity. Not only is this a successful program but leadership has recognized it as so. Finally, at the advanced level, other organizations now use the campaign as a model of communication strategy; it sets the agenda for future campaigns across industry.

Strategic planning is a critical requirement for the PAO's success in advancing the command's communications objectives. Reviewing the two Michaelson and Stacks models presented earlier in this chapter, it is plain to see that public affairs efforts cannot be successful without proactive,

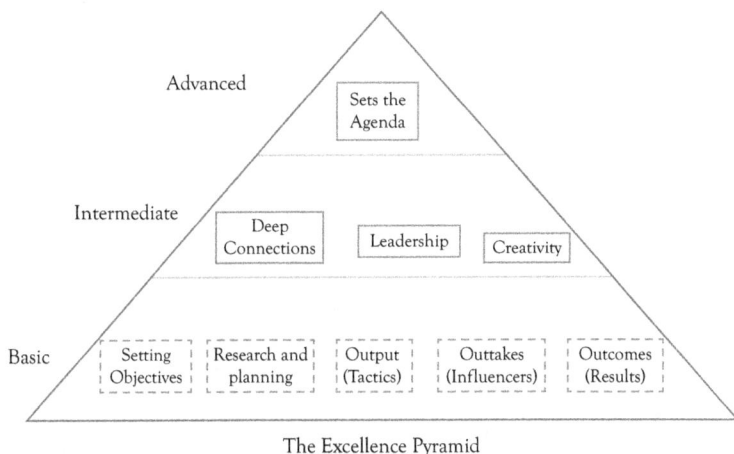

The Excellence Pyramid

Figure 7.3 The Excellence Pyramid[3]

(used with permission).

strategic planning that includes measurable objectives, is grounded in research, and evaluated for return on engagement. It is significant that the first step used in the planning process discussed in this chapter is research. Good research practices focus on asking the right questions of the right stakeholder group and analyzing the data using the right methodology. Anything less is like building your house on sand.

CHAPTER 8

Internal Information

There are three major areas of responsibility for military public affairs communication efforts: internal information, external information, and community relations. Think of them as the three legs of the public affairs target set. The next three chapters will discuss each in turn.

A major difference between civilian public relations and military public affairs is the emphasis on *internal* information. The military's internal stakeholders are arguably one of the military's most important and requires the same or greater attention as the other two legs of the target set. Effective military PAOs and commanders understand that internal communication is not just about passing information to audiences within the organization; it is about building trust and relationships between leadership and subordinates, creating a shared understanding of the organization's goals, values, and guidelines, and forging a sense of community within the organization.[1]

Who Are Our Internal Stakeholders and Why Are They Important?

Officers and enlisted personnel in the service organization (active and reserve) make up the primary stakeholder group. Military personnel are considered spokespersons whenever they are seen in uniform in public and they represent their service at all times through their words and actions. Personnel, especially junior personnel, are often our most credible spokespersons and need to be informed so they understand not only current operations but also the policies and decisions behind those policies.

Civilian employees are another internal stakeholder group that requires attention. While they are typically not as readily identifiable as personnel in uniform, they typically do not deploy and generally stay in one locale over many years. They are in a very real sense the neighbor talking over the fence with other neighbors. Thus, it is important for them to receive the same mission and policy information as their uniformed counterparts. They are also usually the keepers of institutional knowledge and history, which makes them a valuable information resource as well.

Family members form a third critical internal stakeholder group. Open and transparent communication with family members can help alleviate stress and uncertainty about their service members' day-to-day mission and responsibilities. It is also critical to supply them with information during deployments to help them understand the need for operational security and to prevent rumors and misinformation from negatively impacting their already stressful lives in the absence of their spouses and loved ones. It is also important they understand the policies and decisions that affect them and their families.

Family members are also often approached by media for interviews about the impact of military operations on their daily lives. The command needs to equip them with resources, information, and procedures for this eventuality lest the news reporting consists mainly of rumor and innuendo.

The lines between external and internal communication are often blurred, and this fact is a consideration that must always be considered by military communicators. With the proliferation of communication channels, military personnel, civilian employees, and family members are able to obtain information about the organization from any number of outside sources. Every effort must be made such that command information is seen as the first and primary source of official information to at least blunt the impact of contrary information, misinformation, and mal-information.

Channels specific to internal communication include but are not limited to e-mail, newsletters, magazines, face-to-face (town hall meetings, all-hands calls), digital signage, audio and video, and command intranets. Websites have been used to great effect to keep these stakeholders informed. Social media has increasingly become a channel that the internal audience relies on for information. Employee work apps such as Slack have found favor in some commands. Video conferencing software has long been used for secure operational communication but also provide viable platforms for internal information efforts. Other innovative channels include chat boards and messaging apps.

It is especially important to communicate directly with internal audiences in times of crisis. External crisis communications reach internal audiences, but research shows that these internal audiences express discontent in both the quantity and the quality of the information received and, as a result, "construct their own narratives based on assumptions and rumors, as well as on the culture within the unit."[2] This is all the more reason to make the internal audience a priority during a crisis.

CHAPTER 9

External Information

As a tax-funded, government organization, the military must communicate with external audiences on a regular basis in order to earn and maintain the public's trust. Although most day-to-day military operations are quite autonomous and some level of operational security is expected, a lack of transparency can often lead to public inquiry or information gaps. Inquiries force the military to shift from *proactive* communications, meaning the military commander starts the conversation, to *reactive* communications of answering questions on a particular topic (that we may not want or are allowed to talk about). Similar to an academic debate, the first person to speak has the opportunity to define terms and set expectations of a desired outcome, which leaves the military at the mercy of the reporter's familiarity on the topic should they be the first to speak. The *law of primacy* also makes it difficult to challenge whatever is said first, even if it is inaccurate or misleading. Information gaps are missing details that are not provided by the primary source, forcing reporters to find secondary sources to complete their story. Secondary sources vary in credibility and can be eyewitnesses or civilian experts, such as academic professors, former military members, and even celebrities. In short, *reactive communications relinquishes control of the narrative to the media.*

In many cases, proactive and transparent communication will help shape the information environment and allow the military to move freely within the space it created. The goal of being proactive should be to have your direct words echoed, and in effect, endorsed by a media outlet your audience trusts. This is easier said than done because media have individual sets of standards for formatting and overall style. Additionally, each media outlet tries to establish its own approach (or angle) to separate itself from the rest of the pack. Understanding these standards and a keen knowledge of the media industry are vital if you do not want your words paraphrased and possibly misconstrued.

Working With the Media

As you read in Chapter 2, the relationship between the military and the media has a precarious past, filled with frustration and extreme measures on both sides of the microphone. Military commanders must remember that the news is not a free public service; it is a business designed to make money. To do this, news outlets need to reach and maintain a large audience of viewers or readers so they can sell advertising. Since we pay for media services or products such as cable TV, Internet access, or physical print copies of media, many people are led to believe that they (the information consumers) are the customers of news. In fact, the viewers and readers are the product that is sold by the news outlets to their advertisers, who are the actual customers.

When we view the media as a business, we begin to discover why some of our news releases or story "pitches" are covered and others are not. If a story is not covered by the media, that does not necessarily mean that it has no news value and the information should be abandoned. It most likely means that the information did not fit the format, in either style or content, of a particular news outlet. A competent military PAO, or military commander, must know the fundamentals of news media and use that information to create content that will fit a particular format or identify the outlets that would be interested in covering the story.

The following overview is not designed to make anyone a media expert. It is, however, going to provide the basic knowledge needed to manage expectations of how a military commander can reach different audiences and help them select the correct tool for the job.

Types of Media Outlets

The first category of news outlets is what is known as *broadcast media*. It is the quintessential mass media, which means it is designed for large and very general audiences. Traditionally, this includes live network television and news radio stations because they transmit signals over the air. Today this includes a multitude of television programs, including local and national network news, "news magazine" programs, cable news channels, and a variety of news and talk radio shows. Content on broadcast media needs to be highly emotional to retain the attention of the viewer or listener. The most common emotions are fear (cops and courts), excitement (emergencies and sports), anger (politics), and compassion (human interest). A visual element is normally needed to invoke these reactions. The information should also be recent and simple enough that it can be conveyed in a few minutes or less to an audience that is most likely multitasking in the car, at work, or at home. Immediacy is vital; news older than 24 hours is largely ignored in broadcast media.

The next major category is *print media*, which mostly includes newspapers and magazines. Print media range from daily to yearly editions, and their audiences can be as broad as multinational populations or as specific as a small neighborhood or school campus. This allows nearly endless options for what could be considered "news" in terms of the topic or recency of the information. Print content is designed to provide a deeper level of detail, so it is highly effective for information that is new to an audience or something that may lack the emotional response for which the more visual media are looking. While broadcast and digital media can provide impressively large audience numbers, print may be more productive in terms of reaching a specific or key demographic and accomplishing a communications objective.

The last major media category is *digital media*, and it is the most difficult to define because almost every aspect of our daily life crosses over into the digital or online environment. Social media will be covered later in this chapter, so this section will mostly discuss online news outlets. Although most broadcast and print media also operate websites, the content is formatted differently and there is more available online space for smaller stories that do not make the final cut for broadcast or print. In addition, in order to receive information via a broadcast or print outlet, one needs to be watching the right channel at the right time or have a physical copy of the publication in hand. Digital media is usually available online for a longer period of time and can be viewed around the world at any time by anyone with Internet access. This again provides the military commander more options to reach the intended audience.

Communication Tactics

Military public affairs offices use a number of communication tactics to share and disseminate information. Written and visual products, known professionally *as information subsidies*, include news releases, feature stories, photographs, video b-roll, and video vignettes. Personal media engagements include interviews, briefings, and editorial boards. And operational media engagements involve embarking and embedding reporters into military units. Similar to media categories, they all have specific purposes based on what is needed to achieve the communication objective. There is no "one-product-fits-all" solution in public affairs.

Written and visual products allow the military to carefully select or craft the information that will be released. This is a safe approach for sensitive topics or information that could be easily taken out of context. News releases are designed for brief and factual information, and are traditionally used to provide operational status updates, major announcements, or public safety warnings. The main purpose of a news release is to get succinct and complete information to news outlets so they can tell our story without needing further clarification. They may also be used to pique a reporter's interest in the story line as part of a strategic tactic to involve the reporter into working on the story. Feature stories use a personal approach and can be more editorial in nature. Larger news media outlets do not normally reprint feature stories and would prefer to have their reporters write an original article, even if it is on the same topic; hence, a proactive news release to bring the reporter to the PAO to work the story. However, smaller outlets with fewer resources will commonly re-print them as written, simply to have more content for their readers. Imagery should tell a story, evoke an emotion, or provide context to a written product. Imagery intended for television needs to be of the highest possible quality, while online imagery requirements are less restrictive. Regardless of the approach selected, all of them require properly trained personnel with the appropriate resources to produce a product that will successfully compete for valuable airtime and print space.

Personal media engagements are perhaps the most terrifying to most military commanders. These media engagements are high risk but with a large reward. It is a very vulnerable position in which to be placed but can also be extremely effective at building trust and public support. The common one-on-one media interview is the most popular because it allows the reporter to gain a large amount of information in a short period of time directly related to their news story. It should be used when only one or very few outlets are requesting information.

When larger or breaking news stories attract multiple outlets with similar inquiries, a single news briefing (sometimes called a news or press conference) will save time and effort in the release of information. For softer or more complex topics, editorial roundtables provide another avenue to engage directly with media reporters in a professional and controlled environment. There are many variations, but quite simply, editorial roundtables are on-the-record (meaning the principal can be quoted by name) and in-depth conversations between military experts and one or more reporters. The military commander should be familiar and comfortable with personally engaging with the media in these settings. This format can be invaluable during a crisis, which will be discussed later in this chapter.

Social Media

Social media tactics are difficult to write about because the platforms are constantly changing, so most of the information is already outdated prior to publication. However, to keep with the spirit of this book, we will still discuss social media in more general context to help guide a military commander's approach to them.

From a communications standpoint, social media provide organizations with the unique capability to directly communicate with an audience without third-party interference from a TV news producer or print editor. Additionally, most platforms allow for two-way engagements with active audiences in the form of comments, replies, threads, shares, and so on. No other media in broadcast, print, and even most digital outlets enable real-time interactions with external audiences like social media. This can be an extremely valuable resource for a variety of communication needs.

Just like any communications campaign, social media should be a strategic tool to help accomplish an objective. Although it is easy to "shoot from the hip" by uploading photos or a simple message at random times during the week, well-performing social media pages provide something of value to their followers so those followers will return, stay engaged, and share with others. The best practice is to define an audience, determine what value the account can provide them, and then communicate on a regular basis. The value provided to the audience can be anything from simple entertainment to educational information. Once all of this is determined, be consistent and reliable so followers know what to expect when they visit the account.

There are numerous challenges and risks for any organization that chooses to communicate through social media. The largest, and less obvious, challenge is the time commitment and manpower needed to properly curate a social media account and engage with the audience. Social media bring new meaning to the 24-hour news cycle as it connects users from the around the world. Historically, social media algorithms highlight content based on its engagement numbers and the overall activity of the account. This means, if the user is not constantly updating and engaging on the platform, their content will be seen by fewer people. The more obvious challenge is the management of bad actors online who engage in trolling, bots, misinformation, disinformation, malinformation, and hacking. Many civilian companies now have dedicated social media teams to make sure they do not miss valuable opportunities or become the victim of a bad actor online. Military public affairs is slowly following suit but still has a long way to go to fully capitalize on this newer form of communication.

Crisis Communications Cycle

The field of crisis communications encompasses more than the traditional definition of repairing an organization's reputation after a crisis occurs. A more useful approach is to view crisis communications as revolving cycles of communication strategies and tactics that help an organization prepare for and navigate through unfortunate or unexpected events. This cycle includes three phases, which include risk, emergency, and crisis communications. Ultimately, proactive risk and emergency communications will help avoid or minimize the negative impacts of the crisis phase. This is accomplished by managing the public's expectations of what an organization is responsible for before, during, and after an incident occurs. Those expectations, whether accurate or inaccurate, will decide the fate of the organization.

Risk Communications

Every organization operates with a number of *inherent risks* that could potentially become an emergency or crisis. Identifying these risks in advance and actively communicating with key audiences to minimize the negative impact they could cause should be part of the military commander's daily routine. To determine which risks to mitigate, the military commander and PAO should evaluate the probability of a possible event and the potential negative impact it would cause. For example, there is a high probability of a training mission getting canceled or postponed due to an isolated mechanical issue. However, such an occurrence would not likely generate any outrage from the public because mechanical issues are somewhat expected from time to time. Having a crisis communication plan with a holding statement and talking points for this situation may not be worth the effort. At the same time, a Navy ship sunk by an UFO would most certainly have news vans lined up at the pier, but such an event is highly unlikely. We would not expect an UFO attack to actually occur, so just like the canceled training mission, it is probably not worth the effort of a crisis communication plan.

The ultimate goal of risk communications is to set the public's expectations for both how likely the event is to occur and what the military's response or role will be after it happens. This is accomplished by proactively educating the public on the risks that are identified and prioritized by the military commander. To find the balance of a higher probability event with a potentially negative impact, it is more effective to think in general terms. This will save the trouble of preparing for hundreds of possible scenarios, many of which will never happen. One approach is to separate these possible events into three categories of operational mishaps, personnel issues, and "acts of God."

The category of *operational mishaps* includes anything that could go wrong in the line of official duty or during military operations. This could mean aircraft crashes, ship collisions, deaths or serious injuries to military members, civilian casualties in combat, and the like. These events do not need to be catastrophic to pose a risk to the military. A minor mishap in a highly visible or influential area can cause more damage than a deadly or tragic event in a remote location. After a mishap, the public expects the military to take care of the people affected, determine what went wrong, and correct the issue so it will not happen again.

Personnel issues are mostly nonoperational incidents involving a member of the military, either on or off duty, that can negatively affect the organization through association. Many members of the public hold military members to a higher standard, so what may not be a risk to a private company could easily bring discredit to the armed services. These can include relatively minor infractions with the law such as assault, vandalism, petty theft, or drunk driving to more extreme cases of murder, domestic terrorism, or active shooter situations. They can also be unethical or social incidents of embezzlement, discrimination, harassment, or hate crimes. In general, the blame will mostly fall on the individual or individuals involved and not on the military. However, the military will be blamed for trends in behavior, cover-ups, and not holding members accountable.

The last category of *acts of God* is the most difficult to plan for due to the very nature of its classification. Some, such as natural disasters, allow the military commander to create a crisis communication plan based on historical or seasonal events. The possibility of a major natural disaster from extreme weather like hurricanes, tornados, and blizzards to geographic occurrences like earthquakes, mudslides, wildfires, and tsunamis is always lurking just around the corner. Military commanders need to let the public know that they are ready for the disasters and explain what they can or cannot provide during the recovery. It is important to remember that even an incident that occurs without any fault to the military, if mismanaged, could lead to a serious crisis. The public expects the military to be prepared, organized, and calm under pressure. If that is not the public's perception, the military can lose credibility, trust, and support all of which can negatively impact operations.

Emergency Communications

Once an incident occurs, the military commander will no longer be able to conduct risk communications and will need to rely on the trust and expectations that were previously built with the public and stakeholders. During or immediately following an active incident, the military commander must shift to the next phase of *emergency communications*, providing instructing information so that those affected or potentially affected know what to do to protect themselves and their property. Everything will be chaotic, making it extremely challenging to determine the immediate communication actions that need to be taken. Military commanders must prioritize their audiences and focus on the information needed to save lives, livelihoods, and the environment. The impacted area could be hyperlocal to one unit, building, or neighborhood, or widespread throughout a region.

The first priority is people who are in danger. Some may be acutely aware that they are in immediate danger and others may not even know they are in an emergency situation. When people are scared, it is difficult for them to process large amounts of complex information. Providing simple and direct information or instructions will help them more easily reach safety. Once they are safe, you can provide additional information on what to do next.

The second priority is people who are physically safe but are scared. Although they are not in immediate danger, if not addressed, they could panic and either put themselves into danger or make the emergency worse for others. We commonly see this in the form of unnecessary stockpiling of supplies or delaying emergency vehicles by congesting roads. Military commanders should reassure the public that they are safe and tell them how to stay safe.

The third priority is people who are physically safe but angry with either the response, the cause, or the situation in general. This is commonly a very vocal group of people who can potentially divert the responders' attention away from those in actual danger. To mentally process an emergency, many people look to place blame, and this can lead to unwarranted anger toward whomever is available. The priority must remain on the safety of life. When time permits, inform the general public of all the actions taken to manage the emergency. Every minute is critical, and the initial actions of the military commander will determine whether or not an emergency becomes a crisis.

Crisis Communications

During risk communications, the military commander established trust and set expectations with the public, both of which were tested during the emergency communications phase. An incident or event becomes a *crisis* for the military commander when the public's expectations are not met and control of the narrative shifts beyond the military's control. If not acted upon quickly, the organization can lose assets, authority, credibility, or all three.

The immediate action requires the military commander to empathize with those who are suffering and accept responsibility where warranted. This can be very uncomfortable for military commanders, but remember, accepting responsibility does not necessarily mean accepting blame for whatever happened. Responsibility in a crisis is the commitment of the military commander to take decisive actions to make the situation better.

In a crisis, actions speak louder than words, so use action verbs. Whether the military commander is speaking to the media at a press conference or to the community in a town hall, they should avoid abstract verbs such as facilitated, planned, and organized. These are difficult for people to visualize and often fall short in changing public opinion. Find a way to use verbs that convey an accomplishment or physical movement, such as searched, cleaned, and deployed. Thoughts and prayers are not enough to ease suffering. Prove your commitment by taking action to fix the problem and then tell the public what you did by using active and specific verbs.

Just like in emergency communications, the military commander needs to use the right communication method to reach those involved in the crisis. A good practice is to remain on the same medium where the crisis is taking place. This will also help contain the potentially harmful information from spreading. For example, if the outrage is trending on social media, the majority of communications should take place on the same platform. Not all crises call for a press conference or town hall. There is an entire communications tool kit at the military commander's disposal to select the appropriate public affairs products that can be disseminated by the most effective media to reach the intended audience.

CHAPTER 10

Community Relations

Although a large portion of military operations occur in secluded or isolated locations, military commanders must not forget that their bases are part of a surrounding community. Restricted training or operating areas may help keep military members out of the public's view, but our ships sail past coastal communities with restaurants, beaches, and boardwalks. Our jets and helicopters fly over downtown business centers, schools, and neighborhoods. Convoys of military equipment roll down our highways. When the public sees this military equipment pass them by, their opinion of the military will instinctively come to mind. This opinion could be positive or negative, and it most likely depends on their previous interactions with the military.

Being part of a community means the military commander has certain responsibilities and expectations, just as any neighbor would. In the private sector, this is commonly referred to as corporate social responsibility, often shortened to CSR. Many businesses strategically approach CSR by financially sponsoring civic events, youth sport teams, or a multitude of other nonprofit community events. For the military, which must operate within the complex legal space of a government agency, CSR is not that simple. There are many restrictions on how government funds and resources may be used outside of official government business, and these will shape how a military commander "gives back" to the local community. However, one advantage the military has is the resource of dozens, if not hundreds, of able bodies who are authorized to provide many volunteer services in the community.

Each community relations engagement should be publicized to the fullest extent to make sure that work, especially the volunteer efforts of the troops, does not go unnoticed. In order to impact the public's opinion of the military, the public needs to recognize when those military members are working in the community. This can be accomplished in-person by hanging banners or by wearing uniforms or unit t-shirts (as long as they are easily recognizable to civilians). It can also be accomplished through secondary channels, such as social media posts or traditional media engagements. Simple communications can expand the public's awareness of all the good deeds being performed by the local military base, which will help achieve the goal of building that positive opinion.

Creating a Culture of Service

Successful community relations programs require resources. In addition to the able-bodied volunteers previously mentioned, the military commander may still need to provide equipment, facilities, and most importantly, time. There will almost always be a small group of self-motivated military members at each base who will use their own time and resources to engage with the community. However, if the command provides basic opportunities and rewards for their members to engage, the level of participation can drastically increase. Remember, public affairs is a function of command and the tone toward community relations is just as influential as the tone toward safety or operational excellence. Military commanders should lead from the front and support those who follow.

Other than those self-motivated members who are actively volunteering, the majority will need clear opportunities to get involved. Military commanders should dedicate time for community relations during normal working hours. Although some people will simply take advantage of this to get out of work, this is not a "day off." The immediate benefits are the increased number of military members working in the community, while the exposure to this rewarding activity may persuade some to become self-motivated to continue on their own time. Both are beneficial to the community relations program. Taking time during the workday will also help create relationships with groups or organizations that are only open during normal business hours such as schools, food banks, and community kitchens.

Once the opportunities are in place, military commanders need to make sure their members have the right tools for the job. This could literally be tools like shovels and rakes for beach or park clean-ups. Or it could be training on how to engage with younger school groups, techniques on public speaking, or knowledge on how to give better base tours. Few things are more frustrating than not having what you need to get the job done, so military commanders should make the investments to keep their members doing great work out in the community.

For many, community relations activities provide intrinsic rewards and a sense of accomplishment. However, military commanders should look for ways to highlight those who are helping to create a culture of service. Similar to dedicating working hours for community relations, the added benefit of tangible rewards may motivate others to get involved. Apart from formal rewards such as military outstanding volunteer service medals, simple rewards can include improved performance marks, letters of appreciation, extra liberty or leave, and recognition during all-hands or unit meetings.

These command efforts of opportunities, tools, and rewards are all designed to enable military members to participate in the base's community relations program and motivate them to not only stay involved but to advocate on the program's behalf with their peers. Once this happens, the culture of service is more likely to be self-sustaining.

Engaging at All Levels

Building a positive opinion with the public is not as easy as volunteering at a local school and then posting a few photos about it on the base's social media account. Like most relationships, trust and support develop over time. Part of the solution is engaging the public with personnel of all ranks, in a variety of scenarios, covering a range of topics.

The goal for the more basic community relations engagements is to create familiarity and general awareness. Before anything else, the military commander should introduce the base personnel to the public and the public to the base personnel. This is done by creating opportunities for the two groups to interact. Bringing the public to base personnel could be as simple as inviting school or youth groups to base/ship tours or hosting a base open house. This tactic also lets the military commander know who the active members of the public are since they are making the effort to travel to the base and learn about their local military members. Getting base personnel out in the public could involve school visits, presentations at scout or other civic group meetings, or participation at patriotic events such as parades and ceremonies.

These public engagements are just like any other form of communication, so the military commander and PAO need to determine the appropriate spokesperson for the audience. The military members conducting these engagements should range from the junior ranks to more senior and experienced members. Targeting junior members for some programs will help the youth groups connect with people closer to their age and also establishes a sense of ownership for junior members who may still be deciding whether or not to make the military a career. Other occasions will be better suited for more senior members with impressive "stories" and more intricate knowledge of military operations.

As highlighted in the B.A.S.I.C. model presented in Chapter 7, community relations activities such as these help build the communication cycle beyond awareness and start generating public understanding and advocacy. The senior leadership engagements should build-off of the school visits and base tours to generate active support from the larger governing bodies. This could include the signing of memos of agreement to establish long-term partnerships for mentor programs, civic/patriotic event participation, volunteer service, and speaking engagements. These formal partnerships solidify the base as a part of the community so that when the ships sail by, aircraft fly over, or military equipment rolls by, the public will feel a sense of ownership and community pride.

Summary and Discussion

The previous four chapters provided details on the strategic communications planning process as well as on the three critical stakeholder segments that are the principle focus of military public affairs efforts.

Chapter 7 covered the four-step planning process public affairs uses to develop the strategic communications plan. We learned the importance of research and measurement and evaluation, areas that often receive short shrift but are crucial to the success of the campaign. We also discovered how Michaelson and Macleod's best practices model assists during the lifecycle of the planning process. Finally, we looked at the advantages of using Michaelson and Stack's B.A.S.I.C. communication objective measurement model to evaluate whether our communication objectives are being met.

In Chapter 8, we learned that military public affairs prioritizes the importance of communicating with its internal stakeholders to the same degree as external information and community relations. Beyond merely passing along information, internal information is about building trust and relationships between leadership and subordinates, creating a shared understanding of the organization's goals, values, and guidelines, and forging a sense of community within the organization.

Chapter 9 went into detail on communicating with external audiences to earn and maintain the public's trust. Also discussed were the various tactics the PAO and his or her staff use with various channels and stakeholders. The chapter also included details on the crisis communication cycle, including risk, emergency, and crisis communication.

Community relations is the third stakeholder segment important to military public affairs and was covered in Chapter 10. Once again, we saw how the B.A.S.I.C. model presented in Chapter 7 helps community relations build the communication cycle toward advocacy.

Before we go into more depth about the people who practice military public affairs, we need to focus in the following chapter on the breadth and depth of the PAO's responsibilities.

CHAPTER 11

Breadth and Depth of Responsibilities

This chapter will focus on and describe the broad arc of PAO responsibilities. Chapter 12 will go into more details on specific areas of emphasis.

The responsibilities of any public affairs officer will vary depending on the organization they represent and the seniority of the role. Regardless of command or seniority, their responsibilities are somewhat similar to those of their civilian counterparts, albeit without the commercial dimension of many private sector public relations campaigns.

Starting at a macrolevel, scholarly research points out that the typical public relations professional operates in two basic domains: one as a technician and the other as a manager.[1] New and more junior PAOs start out as technicians. PAOs in this role are usually not involved in defining problems and developing solutions but are tacticians who spend the majority of their time writing, producing, and placing communication messages across the various media. Those in this role tend to be creative and talented with language and images. The tactical execution of the public relations plan relies heavily on their competence in creating powerful and persuasive messages. However, as a technician, the PAO rarely has a seat at the management table and does not have a voice in the strategy of the organization. They are brought in once the strategy is set to execute the tactics (deliverables).

Mid-grade to senior PAOs enact the manager role. As a communications manager, the PAO will have the broad responsibility of organizing and integrating communication activities. They are strategists with their "finger on the pulse" of internal and external perceptions of the command and the command's activities. They are responsible for planning and executing communication strategies that align messages and support the commander's intent. Evaluation and measurement are essential to this planning and execution. The resulting data help inform better decisions for managing these strategies, which helps the command better achieve its mission. In the manager role, the PAO is also responsible for monitoring an organization's external environment, constantly scanning for issues that might impact the command, such as policies and legislation, and ensuring the command is able to meet the needs of its stakeholders.[2]

A principal responsibility for all PAOs is to serve as the commander's communication adviser. As such, they must have a place at the decision-making table. This is best facilitated if they are a member of the commander's personal staff. In this position, they are responsible for providing communication advice and counsel at the tactical, operational, and strategic levels. This includes anticipating and advising the commander on the possible effects of military operations and command activities on stakeholder perceptions and actions.

The role of an adviser extends beyond external communication. The PAO must also counsel the commander on the internal communication ramifications and perceptions of policies and procedures. PAOs also provide advice on the public affairs requirements of mission execution.

Closely related to the function of communication adviser is the responsibility PAOs have to prepare commanders, senior staff, and family members to speak with the media and the public. This is especially important with regard to preparing members of the command who might be asked to represent the organization at public meetings, be interviewed by the media as subject matter experts, or interact with the public as part of the command's community relations activities. Preparation responsibilities range from media training for commanders and others in the command to facilitating media and public engagements. Facilitating these events includes tasks such as securing and setting up the venue, ensuring all materials for both the principal and the public are prepared and available, timing of sending invitations to the event, and other similar details.

Another important responsibility is engaging with the media. In the media relations role, the PAO is responsible for developing a working relationship with reporters and other media representatives, both foreign and domestic. This includes handling any media requests for information and comment, developing messaging strategies, responses to query and public statements, and evaluating the success of each evolution post event (see Chapter 8).

Post-event evaluation is where the measurement and evaluation skills of the PAO are particularly valuable. Through research and monitoring, the PAO is able to keep abreast of key performance indicators (KPIs), such as mentions of the command in the media and across digital platforms and brief the commander on external and internal perceptions of the command.

In all cases, this also includes coordinating information with the appropriate staff and agencies prior to release. The PAO plays an important role in mitigating misinformation and disinformation and deterring our adversaries; interagency cooperation and coordination are key to this role.

In a similar vein, it is the PAO's responsibility to prepare information related to unit participation in military operations, reaction to local, regional, and world events, and the command's environmental efforts. The PAO is also responsible for the security and policy review of materials such as speeches, news articles, and radio and television show participation. In addition, this review needs to ensure integration with the objectives of the command and higher headquarters.

The PAO often writes speeches and ghost-writes for the commander and senior staff. This involves researching, planning, and implementing communications strategies that balance informative *storytelling* with the protection of national security interests. It also goes hand-in-hand with the responsibility to assist commanders in developing the right communications strategy for internal and external stakeholders.

The PAO leads the command's public affairs staff in all communication planning, execution, and assessment efforts ensuring the commander's intent is communicated in aligned messages, actions, and visual documentation in all internal and external communications. A major part of that responsibility is overseeing projects involving writing, photography, videography, and graphic design produced by enlisted public affairs specialists, such as command/base/unit newspapers, radio and television programming, magazines, internal information materials, and social media content (see Chapter 9).

Finally, PAOs act as a liaison with Hollywood, actively courting film studios through Entertainment Liaison Offices based in Los Angeles (as an example, the Navy Office of Information West). These PAOs have an intimate understanding of the needs and requirements of film and television production. Married with their understanding of military culture and operations, the PAO is able to help the production company get the necessary assistance from the military so that its portrayals are both realistic and accurate, while protecting the taxpayers' investment in the Armed Forces. Similar offices in New York assist the major news networks and the magazine industry.

Summary

In summary, the public affairs officer's communication skills should be used to bridge communication gaps and foster transparent and effective communication among staff sections/departments and subordinate units. Communication is key to morale, command cohesiveness, and mission accomplishment.

PART IV

The People Who Practice Military Public Affairs

This part defines who military PAOs are, how they differ from civilian public relations professionals, and outlines the range of their communication responsibilities. We will illuminate how PAOs learn the tools of public relations as practiced within the military environment. Chapter 14 explains the qualifications of and accession into the profession by service. This part concludes with an overview of how PAOs are typically employed.

PART IV

The People Who Preserve
Military Public Affairs

CHAPTER 12

Who Are Military PAOs?

Effective Communicator

Military PAOs are, first and foremost, effective communicators. As described in Cutlip and Center's *Effective Public Relations*, they are able to establish priorities, define publics, set goals and objectives, and develop messages, strategies, and tactics.[1] Beyond the ability to plan strategically, a military PAO must be able to plan laterally with other departments within their organization as well as with stakeholders ranging from adjacent units to other entities such as the Department of State and other government and nongovernment organizations. Additionally, military public affairs efforts must nest vertically within the strategic planning of their military service, the National Military Strategy, the National Defense Strategy, and the National Security Strategy in order to achieve a mutually beneficial end.

Military Public Affairs Versus Public Relations

Although military public affairs and public relations exhibit some differences and unique coordination issues, military public affairs and public relations can both abide by the definition of public relations presented in Cutlip and Center's *Effective Public Relations*, "Public relations is the management function that establishes mutually beneficial relationships between an organization and the publics on whom its success or failure depends."[2] Public relations and public affairs share values outlined in ethical codes or principles, such as advocacy, honesty, loyalty, and fairness. [3, 4]

Each military service similarly describes the role their professional communicators play. For example, the Marine Corps states that public affairs "plans, coordinates and implements communication strategies designed to build understanding, credibility, trust and mutually beneficial relationships with the domestic and foreign publics on whom the Marine Corps' success or failure ultimately depends," calling itself "a liaison between Marines and the public" and concluding that "in peacetime and in war, the public affairs mission is to inform America's citizens about what their Marines are doing."[5]

Although the naming convention of these communication functions may seem purely semantic, military public affairs and public relations do have some differences.[6] The difference in title between public relations and public affairs stems from a desire to thwart any affiliation with laws prohibiting government spending on publicity unless explicitly authorized by Congress. This is a notable difference between military public affairs and public relations—military public affairs is "restricted from and does not try to influence public opinion."[7] Military public affairs is also unique in that it serves an internal communication role typically taken care of by human resources in the civilian sector. Additionally, as it pertains to the practice of research, military PAOs are not permitted to survey the U.S. public while their civilian public relations counterparts can.

In practice, military PAOs face certain unique coordination issues. The military rank structure and hierarchy among organizations can be both helpful and hurtful as PAOs work to gain a seat at the decision-making table with the leadership. PAOs are often the most junior members of the staff on which they serve, which can be a hindrance in a rank-based organization. Communication efforts may be undermined if trust and confidence in the PAO's expertise in the communication field has not been accepted by those in a position to make decisions. However, the converse is also true. In the instance that public affairs is included as a key contributor in strategic planning, the advocacy by decision makers on behalf of coordinated communication efforts can be the most influential asset in an organization that respects and responds to rank.

Unlike some larger public relations firms, a military public affairs shop typically has little to work with by way of budget, due in part to its lack of an advertising or publicity function. In addition to some prohibitions against surveying the American public directly, a subordinate public affairs shop will likely not have the funding available to commission internal survey research prior to a campaign plan.

Classification, operational security, logistics, transportation, and safety—often in a combat zone—are additional obligations of a military PAO, particularly when working with embedded media or communicating about ongoing military operations. For example, during a media embed involving the departure of all Marines from Helmand Province, Afghanistan, the PAO ensured each reporter agreed to an embargo—to hold the release of their stories—until the final flight had touched down at the end location. The stakes were very high in this environment because the reporters had the information and ability to compromise a sensitive and dangerous troop movement with the potential to put lives at risk. The public affairs team in this instance needed to be well-versed in the classification of various materials and operational elements so that they could build and maintain strong relationships and communicate messages to external media without compromising the operational security of the base and military forces.

Marketing

Each service relies on marketing and advertising to recruit, train, and retain quality individuals to serve in the armed forces. While the military services carry out this function differently, there is a relationship between marketing and public affairs.

The services' marketing and advertising functions are primarily responsible for the management and dissemination of a Congressionally determined budget that is used for events, mailing lists and rosters, and recruitment tools and capabilities. Public affairs works in tandem with marketing and advertising, as they are responsible for communicating the mission of the services to the external audience through visual and written means, such as social and traditional news media or community relations activities.

Operations in the Information Environment

As an information-related capability, public affairs needs to work collaboratively with other Department of Defense activities in the information space to ensure the ability to accomplish the mission while maintaining trust and credibility. While concurrent involvement is imperative, the purposes of military information operations and public affairs are different. Joint *Publication 3-13 Information Operations* states that information-related capabilities are used "to gain advantages in the information environment, just as they would use more traditional military technologies to gain advantages in other operational environments."[8] Using information operations in support of lines of effort to combat an enemy puts different legal and ethical factors into play in terms of the command's communication efforts. While public affairs plays a strategic role in the battlespace, public affairs is bound by laws and ethical principles that demand truth and transparency for the citizens of our nation.

Public affairs is charged with providing timely, truthful, and accurate information so that the public has the facts to make informed decisions. Information operations, on the other hand, serves to complement operations in order to "influence, disrupt, corrupt, or usurp the decision making of adversaries and potential adversaries while protecting our own."[9]

In their efforts to counter adversary propaganda, misinformation, mal-information and disinformation, and prevent deception by the enemy, public affairs and information operations need to be on the same sheet of music. However, public affairs and information operations have different laws regarding the international population and the domestic population, as well as what must be communicated and for what reasons. As specified in the *Principles of Information*, public affairs has an obligation to provide truthful information to the American public. Information operations, however, is permitted in certain instances to deliberately influence specified foreign audiences through the release of select information. This may include deliberate deception for the purpose of targeting adversaries in order to affect their decision-making processes. With respect to public affairs and communication with foreign or domestic publics, such behavior is specifically prohibited by the *Principles of Information*.

Maintaining the credibility of the public affairs office as a source of truth is imperative. Public affairs may coordinate factual information with operations in the information environment for the purposes of various information related capabilities' collective situational awareness, deconfliction, and collaboration. For example, during a deployment, a working group meeting with other entities operating in the information environment facilitated a broader understanding of the multitude of players in the information space. Collaboration between public affairs and information operations synchronized objectives and helped build a better understanding of how various actions supported mission accomplishment.

Adviser, Spokesperson, Liaison, and Leader

Similar to the civilian practice of public relations, these day-to-day activities and breadth of experiences of a military PAO vary. Cutlip and Center's *Effective Public Relations* lists the following 11 categories of the responsibilities of public relations specialists: "writing and editing, media relations and social media, research, management of clients and staff, strategic planning, counseling, special events, speaking, production, training, and (maintaining) personal contacts."[10]

While these categories also encompass the roles and responsibilities of a military PAO, the different "billets" or jobs throughout an officer's military career present varying opportunities to exercise each of these roles. Four roles of particular importance in the military context are those of adviser, spokesperson, liaison, and leader. According to *Joint Publication 3-61 Public Affairs*, the PAO serves as the principal spokesperson and senior public affairs adviser for the commander—leading, coordinating, and aligning all communication activities and providing counsel to leaders within the command.[11] The PAO also liaises with internal and external stakeholders, deconflicting and synchronizing within the organization and ensuring pertinent, timely, and accurate information is shared with the stakeholders.

Leadership is a hallmark of any officer rank in the public relations specialty. Prior to training and qualification to serve in the public affairs specialty, officers in every service first go through a service-specific leadership development program. A military PAO has many roles and responsibilities, but the training and mentoring of subordinates and effective management of their public affairs shops are viewed as a primary duty. Chapter 14 discusses the breadth of assignments carried out by PAOs.

Communication Leader

Military public affairs officers are leaders with a trained vision for both opportunistic and consequential outcomes resulting from communications. While the roles and responsibilities are clearly defined for a PAO, the ability for these individuals to identify second- and third-order effects of a commander's decision making and its relation to perception and communication is paramount to mission success. This is true in both times of normal operations and in times of crisis. PAOs often are required to support this mission in austere or even communication restrictive environments, such as isolated forward operating bases in a combat zone or naval vessels at sea with limited communications connectivity. An understanding of the operational and security environments in which the unit is operating is needed for sound judgment and execution of the public affairs support to the overall mission.

Similar to a director of communications of a corporate organization or a component of one, an effective military communication leader regularly practices and weighs the consequences or benefits of decisions, not just communication activities. The mindset of a PAO is forward-thinking and expands beyond the command or installation itself. An essential skill emphasized and practiced in a PAO's initial training is the ability to make predictive outcomes and not to be bound by circumstances but to instead ask essential questions about what can be done with the resources available and how communications could be a part of the solution to a problem.

PAOs have the responsibility not only to provide advice and counsel ahead of or in response to decisions that impact the organizational narrative but also to lead teams, both large and small, to orchestrate that narrative in a transparent and methodical manner. Service public affairs offices are postured in such a way that the PAO has a direct line to an installation commander as part of the command's immediate support team. In addition to supporting and providing guidance to a commander and their staff, a PAO also aligns their own public affairs team with the commander's priorities, vision, and goals. This two-way communication leadership must be timely, thorough, and organized to effectively target and produce the right communication activities at the right time, to the right audience.

At the forefront of a PAO's mind is the organization's mission, vision, and priorities. In order to lead the communication effort for an installation or during a deployment, the PAO must adopt this same vision and support it with achievable and measurable public affairs objectives. Similarly, a commander's problem or issue is also at the forefront of a PAO's mind, in an effort to be part of the solution through communication efforts.

While a PAO's focus is on communication, it is noteworthy that their understanding of and relationships with units across a command are essential and are not just surface level. A PAO must always be in-tune with the pulse of their command and the people in it, in order to maintain a high level of awareness in the event of an emergency or crisis. This understanding is a product of internal relationships and trust-building among commanders, subordinate commanders, senior enlisted leaders, and more.

In the world of military public affairs, PAOs aim to not just have a *seat* at the decision-making table among top leadership but have a *voice* at that table. A communication leader is not a "break glass in case of emergency" fix. A communication leader builds the relationships, the strategies, and the objectives to consistently advise or influence mission execution or problem-solving.

Summary

This chapter provided an overview of the similarities and differences between military affairs and civilian public relations. We reviewed the roles of particular importance to the PAO in the military context, those being marketer, adviser, spokesperson, liaison, and communications leader. We also summarized how public affairs operates in the "information operations" environment, in an attempt to promote an understanding of the PAO's role in that space.

CHAPTER 13

Education and Training

As with any professional position, the PAO must learn not only the organizational mission, vision, and goals but also must learn the tools of the trade as practiced within the military environment. This involves various schools and programs that correspond to the various levels of practice the PAO will practice in. Most PAOs begin their communication careers by completing a course of study at the Defense Information School. Upon graduation from DINFOS and at points throughout their career, they may attend further schools to continue their education, often in concert with a university, school, or department of communication.

Defense Information School

Education and training for all of the Department of Defense (DoD) photography, videography, and communication take place at the Defense Information School (DINFOS) at Fort George G. Meade, Maryland. In 1998, the last of the DoD schools teaching communications skills was consolidated at DINFOS creating a single school for training service members in communication, public affairs, and visual information specialties.[1] This chapter will outline the formal communications training currently offered at DINFOS.

DINFOS Public Affairs and Communication Strategy Qualification Course (PACS-Q)

Public Affairs and Communication Strategy Qualification Course (PACS-Q) is a 45-day course that provides entry-level public affairs training for the Department of Defense, U.S. government agencies, and selected foreign military professionals. Instruction focuses on the foundational elements of the communication planning process, principles, and techniques associated with implementing effective communication strategies, and the processes involved in integrating communication into military planning and operations.[2] According to the Defense Information School, graduates of PACS-Q are qualified to perform the basic duties of a public affairs practitioner.

Core Elements

PACS-Q is an updated version of DINFOS' officer and senior enlisted training and qualification course, which was called Public Affairs Qualification Course (PAQC) prior to October 2020. The updated course organizes all instruction and evaluation under five focus areas agreed upon by representatives from the Army, Air Force, Marine Corps, Navy, and Coast Guard:

1. provide communication strategy counsel to command and higher headquarters;
2. leverage relationships with the command, the community, the media, partners, and stakeholders (influencers) to accomplish a mission;
3. employ a communication team in accordance with DoD policies and tactics, techniques, and procedures to achieve commander's desired end state;
4. communicate in steady-state and event driven scenarios in order to accomplish missions;
5. provide communication tactics in alignment with the commander's desired state and higher-level guidance.

Critical thinking, planning, and tactics are taught using realistic scenarios that provide an opportunity for students to practice and hone their new skills with the coaching and mentorship of military and civilian faculty. Upon completion of PACS-Q, a graduate understands their role within a nuanced military staff and is able to plan, advise, and lead in a complex information environment.[3]

DINFOS Intermediate Courses

Joint Intermediate Public Affairs Course (JIPAC)

Following completion of PACS-Q, and with experience in public affairs leadership and practice in field and/or fleet environments, PAOs attend the Defense Information School's Joint Intermediate Public Affairs Course (JIPAC), where they expand on communication leadership skills and venture deeper into concepts and practices of strategic thinking and planning capabilities. This intermediate-level course serves PAOs and senior enlisted public affairs service members with approximately 4–10 years of experience. Generally, public affairs officers are serving in deputy or lead roles by the time they attend JIPAC.

Topic areas of JIPAC expand beyond tactics within operations and reshape the public affairs thought process. During simulated exercises, PAOs practice communication research, analysis and planning, strategic foresight, understanding information disorder, interorganizational cooperation, cultural influences, and informational power, and more. Multiple layers of communication capabilities are combined to drive strategic thinking and emphasize data-driven planning. The course and objectives support critical Department of Defense doctrine. By course completion, students fulfill the outcome of assisting the Joint Force to "maintain the competitive advantage in the information environment through communication professionals who think strategically to conduct and apply research, planning and analysis; operationalize communication capabilities; and merge communication with military operational art."[4]

Combat Camera Leadership Course

As PAOs progress in their careers, some are assigned to Combat Camera units and require specific skillsets to perform as combat camera planners. The Defense Information School leads this effort with the Combat Camera Leadership Course (CCLC) that trains selected officers and noncommissioned officers in the principles, techniques, and skills required. The training focuses on three primary areas: combat camera orientation, deployment preparedness, and field operations. In this course,

PAOs learn to operate within the mission and functions of combat camera, including the development of operational support plans, policy, procedures, and imagery management plans. The course also provides in-depth theoretical and working knowledge of how combat camera functions within the Department of Defense.[5]

As the training pivots to deployments and contingency operations in the field, PAOs experience having to respond to a request for forces and prepare a communications portion of an operations order. They are tested on working through a given scenario to organize themselves with equipment, technology, operating within the current policies, acquiring imagery, leading their teams, and holistically supporting the commander's operational objectives. Finally, students deliver field-reporting requirements including a situation report and an after-action report.[6]

In addition to JIPAC and CCLC, the Defense Information School also offers a Visual Information Course, where PAOs and senior enlisted non-commissioned officers learn to manage visual information operations. The course focuses on doctrine and ethics, visual information resource management, and accessioning and copyright, and visual information strategic planning. Students learn imagery accessioning, collection and dissemination to both internal and external customers, DoD policy and compliance on image editing of official DoD imagery, and imagery release policy. The content presented in the course allows PAOs to pair visual information planning and tactics with strategic goals in support of contingencies, joint operations, information operations, and combat camera operations.[7]

Collectively, DINFOS' intermediate courses challenge and elevate PAO baseline skills and knowledge to broaden strategic planning and communication leadership capabilities to support the commander's vision, mission, and goals. The faculty focuses on current scenarios and curating the most realistic exercise environments to induce the complexity of leading, planning, and decision making required of a PAO.

DINFOS Advanced Courses

Joint Contingency Public Affairs Course (JCPAC)

Following completion of JIPAC, officers and senior enlisted noncommissioned officers in the public affairs career field attend the Defense

Information School's advanced Joint Contingency Public Affairs Course aimed at expanding the PAO's strategic foresight in a Joint military service environment. This course is a realistic stress test played out in an exercise mimicking a joint staff scenario. Role players create an environment that challenges student confidence and competence in infusing communication into operational planning so PAOs can demonstrate their skillsets.

JCPAC instruction includes training in joint planning, communication research and analysis, strategic foresight, issues management, information disorder, operationalizing public affairs and communication strategy in a contingency environment, providing communication counsel to senior leaders, and assessing communication effectiveness. The fast-moving course exercise intertwines complex issues and narratives with opportunities to employ rapid planning and problem-solving, while also navigating fluid changes and dynamic relationships. PAOs make recommendations to the joint staff and the commander, exercise the skills of an effective staff officer, and engage with key stakeholders in the most realistic setting provided by senior subject matter experts in operations, intelligence, civil affairs, information operations, and other disciplines that fall into operational art and design.[8]

DINFOS Technical Training

In addition to communication qualification and leadership courses, DINFOS provides entry-level through advanced training for technical skills. These technical courses teach the skills required for a "communication technician" as described in Cutlip and Center's *Effective Public Relations* but also focuses heavily on communication through visual information specialties.[9]

The entry-level course for enlisted communicators from all services is called Mass Communication Foundations (MCF). It teaches students to apply the fundamentals of journalistic writing, still photography, videography, digital graphic design, and interactive multimedia fundamentals of English and journalism to news and narrative stories, captions, and video scripts for use in both internal and external communication products.[10]

Based on their service's requirements, students in these courses will go on to specialize in fields such as broadcast journalism, graphic design, photography, videography, and writing. Follow-on intermediate and advanced courses include further specialization in technical skills, such as the digital multimedia course, as well as the Intermediate Public Affairs Specialist Course, which teaches the communication manager skillset as more senior service members transition from a predominantly technical role to a more managerial one.[11]

DINFOS Online Learning

PAVILION
Another DINFOS initiative for the training and sustainment of communication professionals who support the Department of Defense is PAVILION: an online public affairs and visual information resource. PAVILION was designed to support an ever-evolving body of best practices for a user population that is dispersed worldwide often with little access to follow-on, in-person training.

Launched in 2020, PAVILION was implemented as a virtual learning tool that expanded upon the DINFOS mission to train communicators within the Department of Defense. It provides trusted resources that are accessible in any clime and place and that are specifically "curated, developed and pulled from training courses, fleet and field and industry as well as crowd sourced from the DoD community of users" to ensure timeliness and relevance of the products provided to users. These resources include checklists, templates, case studies, exercises, and modules that support the vast responsibilities and requirements of military communicators. [12]

Graduate Education

Outside of DINFOS, some mid-level officers (those ranging from approximately 8 to 12 years in service) are rigorously selected to attend public relations and communications graduate degree programs as part of their service's career progression and talent management initiatives. The programs available to public affairs officers vary by service. While similar, the programs available often differ in length and focus, with some leaning more toward a focus on research and others toward corporate communication.

One such program is San Diego State University's Public Affairs Officer program, which began in 2004. Designed to provide the academic basis for a strategically oriented public affairs program, this accelerated 10-month Mass Communication and Media Studies master's degree program yields "strategic analytic skills that permit them to plan public affairs programs with measurable outcomes, implement those programs, and measure their effectiveness" to provide the strategic communication counsel critical for their commanders' success.[13]

Another available program is the Army's Advanced Civil School (ACS) at Georgetown University. This is an 18-month program through which officers earn a master's degree in Public Relations and Corporate Communications. The Navy participates in a similar program of study at Georgetown as well.[14]

The Air Force has an additional professional development program apart from DINFOS. The Education with Industry (EWI) Program is a

> … highly selective, competitive, career development program designed to improve the technical, professional, and management competencies of participating students by partnering with top tier public and private sector companies. During the 10-month tour, students embed with an industry team to meet their specific career desired learning objectives. Through hands on exposure to industry best practices, students develop the necessary competencies, skills, knowledge, and abilities to build, sustain and retain a mission-ready workforce, as well as learn how to better partner with industry in the future.[15]

Summary

In this chapter, we sought to illuminate the numerous professional development opportunities available to the PAO. Initial training begins at the Defense Information School, which also offers intermediate and advanced professional development courses. Advanced education typically includes public relations and communications graduate degree programs as part of each service's career progression and talent management initiatives. The programs available to PAOs vary by service but each provides graduate level education in strategic communications, including the counseling skills critical for their commanders' success.

CHAPTER 14

Public Affairs Specialty Qualification and Accession

PAOs enter into the military communications career field from varied educational backgrounds via a commissioning source. Commissioning sources include Officer Training School, United States Service Academies, or the Reserve Officers' Training Corps. Typically, PAOs are commissioned officers and have a four-year college degree. Many have postgraduate degrees, especially mid-grade, and senior officers.

Other avenues of entry might also include seasoned enlisted communication specialists selected for commissioning, warrant officers, or selective or required lateral transfers from other career fields. For some services, PAOs can go directly into the career field as a newly commissioned second lieutenant or ensign, and for other services, commissioned officers are laterally transferred as part of the structure of their service's professional development and may begin their public affairs duties at a company-grade officer level after approximately 5–10 years of service.

Army Qualifications and Accession

Public affairs is considered a "functional area" in the U.S. Army (FA 46). Army public affairs officers begin their careers in one of the Army's accessions branches (Combat Arms, i.e., Infantry, Air Defense Artillery, Armor, Aviation, Corps of Engineers, Field Artillery, and Special Forces) and attend branch basic and advanced courses. Success in company-grade assignments is a perquisite to selection to the public affairs functional area and usually occurs in the eighth year of service. Early functional designation for a few highly qualified and successful officers is possible in their fourth year of commissioned service. As with the other services, designation is based upon the needs of the army, officer preference, military experience, and in some cases, civil schooling. They continue to wear their branch insignia throughout their career.[1]

Most officers will not receive an FA 46 assignment until selection to major and functional designation as a PAO. The Army seeks to ensure that an officer's first FA 46 assignment to be a position where the officer is personally supervised or mentored by a senior PAO and works with public affairs noncommissioned officers.[2]

The most competitive officers are those who have served successfully as the PAO in operational units. Prior to their first FA 46 assignment, all officers must attend the Defense Information School's Public Affairs Qualification Course (PAQC).[3]

FA 46 captain positions are key developmental billets. At this level, officers can serve as public affairs detachment commanders, mobile public affairs detachment team leaders, or division or higher public affairs staff officers.[4]

FA 46 majors serve primarily in operational PA assignments and "should aggressively seek key assignments in which they are the principal spokesperson for operational units or mobile public affairs detachment commanders."[5] Other desirable assignments include nominative assignments on headquarters, DoD, and joint staffs. "Majors who have successfully served in BCTs as the spokesperson for and principal advisor to the commander on public affairs operations are highly sought after for future senior leadership positions including division and corps PAO."[6]

Public affairs lieutenant colonels are generally assigned to senior staff positions, where they can fully use their knowledge of the Army and their functional area. Highly competent PAOs with demonstrated high potential are typically assigned to flag-officer level commands and nominative positions on headquarters, DoD and joint staffs, and Defense Media Activity/Armed Forces Radio and Television Service (DMA/AFRTS) network command positions. Joint assignments are highly desirable in order for the officer to gain joint and combined command exposure and experience.[7]

A graduate degree in a public affairs-related discipline is highly desired, but not required, for promotion to colonel. In addition, PAOs are encouraged to seek professional accreditation through organizations such as the Public Relations Society of America or the International Association of Business Communicators.[8]

All FA 46 colonels need to complete resident or nonresident Senior Service College. As the senior professionals in their functional area, they serve primarily on joint, ACOM, ASCC, or HQDA staffs. Key assignments include combatant commands and ACOM or ASCC Public Affairs officer positions, director of Army Broadcasting Service, director of Army Public Affairs Center, director of the Defense Information School, or division chief billets on the HQDA and DOD public affairs staffs.[9]

Public affairs units and officers routinely support joint operations, and at some point, officers will serve in joint commands whether or not they are formally assigned to a JDAL position. Officers assigned to JDAL positions must meet all JPME requirements. Graduation from the Joint and Combined Warfighting School prior to a follow-on joint assignment is required for designation as Joint Specialty Officers (skill identifier 3L). FA 46 officers normally will not be considered for assignment to JDAL positions until they have served an initial Army FA 46 assignment and been selected for promotion to major.[10]

Navy Qualifications and Accession

The Navy rarely accesses personnel directly into the public affairs specialty. Most will be selected as a lateral transfer from another warfare community, which generally occurs at four-to-six years of service.

Direct Commissioning

The direct commissioning process begins with an application. Military and/or civilian work experience should mirror fields desirable for the specialty (broadcasting, communications, English, journalism, marketing, public relations, speech, or related field).[11]

As part of the application, the candidate for direct commissioning must submit to three interviews. At least one interview must be conducted by a Navy active duty, reserve, or retired PAO in the paygrades of 0–5 or above. The second interview must be conducted by a Navy active duty PAO in the paygrades of 0–4 or above. The third interview may be conducted by any Navy officer in the paygrades of 0–5 or above. Candidates can increase their competitiveness by including endorsements by senior officers or senior enlisted, active duty, reserve or retired, with their application. Candidates must score a minimum of 40 on the officer aptitude rating.[12]

Finally, direct commission applicants must submit a portfolio that includes but is not limited to stories, photographs, speeches, communication plans, and/or marketing material.[13]

Lateral Transfer

New navy PAOs must have extensive corporate (Fleet) knowledge and experience before applying to laterally transfer into the public affairs specialty. Applicants for lateral transfer into public affairs have to be in the grade of Lieutenant Commander or below, possess at least a baccalaureate degree, and have served a minimum of 24 months of commissioned service. A warfare qualification is desirable but not a requirement. Likewise, prior experience in a public affairs billet, or as a collateral duty PAO, is encouraged but not required for a lateral transfer request.[14]

Candidates for lateral transfer must also submit a portfolio including, but not limited to, stories, photographs, speeches, communication plans, and/or marketing material. They must also submit a proposed response plan to a public affairs scenario assigned by the PAO community manager. These response plans should utilize the Research, Plan, Implement, Evaluate (RPIE) model to address the scenario.[15]

The typical competitive selectee has between four and six years of excellent service as a commissioned officer, is warfare qualified, and is career motivated. Most have experience as collateral-duty PAOs or possess an educational background in mass communication, journalism, or a related field.

Navy PAOs attend DINFOS for basic public affairs training. Initial assignments for Navy PAOs are chosen carefully, with the most proficient personnel assigned to the most difficult jobs. It should be noted that although Navy PAOs are expected to be ready to perform their jobs once they arrive in the Fleet, they have a strong support structure in place throughout the world that is basically a secondary public affairs chain of command that can assist the junior PAO.[16] Figures 14.1, 14.2, and 14.3 are taken from the "2020 Public Affairs Career Progression Brief"[17] and illustrate both the expectations and career path for Navy PAOs following entry into the public affairs community.

Marine Corps Qualifications and Accession

Marine Corps officer accession begins at the company-grade level upon completion of Officer Candidate School (OCS) and The Basic School (TBS). TBS, a mandatory, 26-week course of instruction required of all newly commissioned second lieutenants, provides the officer with a broad knowledge of the Marine Corps, focused on Infantry. The Basic School is an experience common to all Marine Corps officers. While at TBS, officers are evaluated in areas such as leadership, military skills, academics, and physical fitness. The Basic School instruction prepares Marine Corps officers to function as basic infantry platoon commanders in the operating forces, no matter what other occupational specialty the Marine focuses on during his or her career. Each Military Occupational Specialty has its own training pipeline. After graduating TBS, students move on to their MOS schools and then out to the Fleet Marine Force or Supporting Establishment.

The United States Marine Corps made significant changes to the organization and naming convention of its public affairs occupational field in 2017 and 2018 in order to increase the Marine Corps' effectiveness in operating within the contested and complex information environment. In October 2017, the 43XX public affairs and 46XX combat camera occupational fields merged into a single 45XX occupational field. The occupational field was designated Communication Strategy and Operations (CommStrat), and the officers in this field are now referred to as CommStrat officers instead of as PAOs. The capabilities of the combined occupational fields were designed to seamlessly integrate with all other joint and warfighting functions and elements of the Marine Air Ground Task Force and supporting establishment and enhance support for operational and institutional objectives. The merger yielded an increased capability

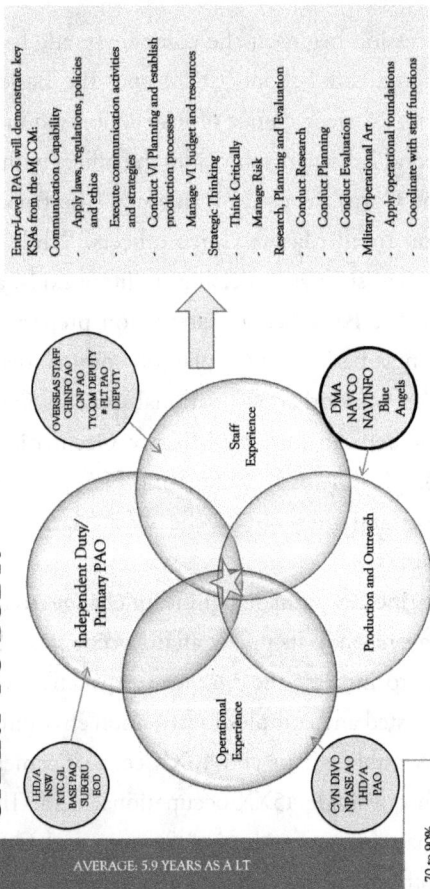

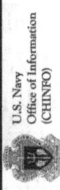

Figure 14.1 The Chart to LCDR

Source: Public Domain, www.mynavyhr.navy.mil/Career-Management/Detailing/Officer/Pers-44-Staff-RL/Public-Affairs/

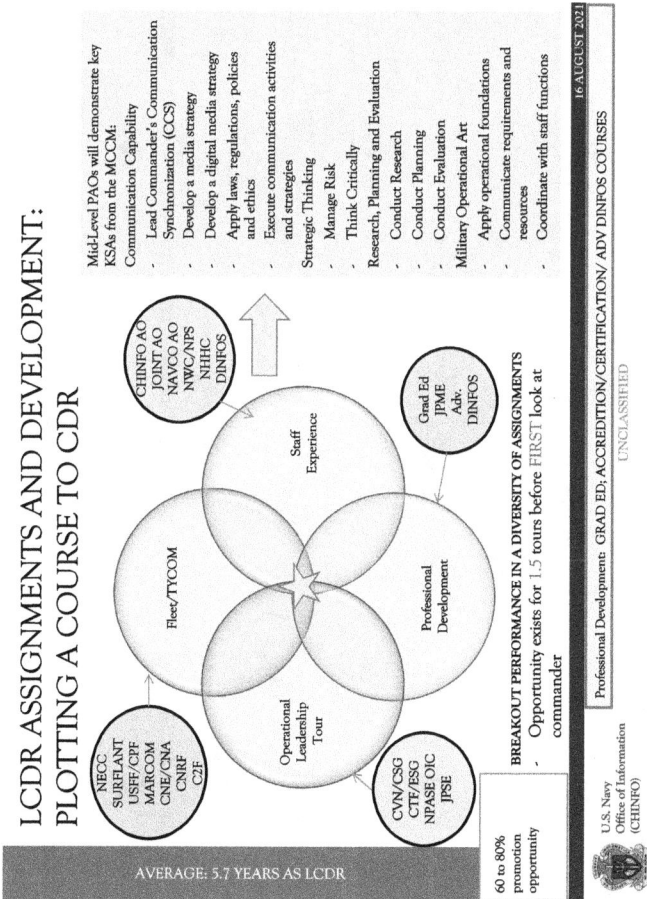

Figure 14.2 The Chart to CDR

Source: Public Domain, www.mynavyhr.navy.mil/Career-Management/Detailing/Officer/Pers-44-Staff-RL/Public-Affairs/

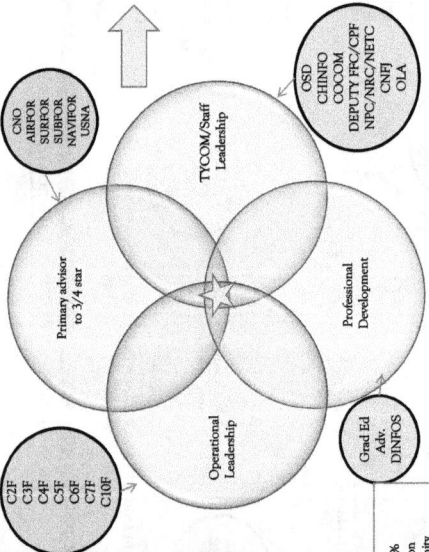

Figure 14.3 The Chart to CAPT

Source: Public Domain, www.mynavyhr.navy.mil/Career-Management/Detailing/Officer/Pers-44-Staff-RL/Public-Affairs/

and capacity to plan and execute communication operations in both the operating forces and supporting establishment, enhancing service-level situational awareness, command and control, and the overall ability to plan for and respond to opportunities in the information environment.

Another way the Marine Corps accesses new CommStrat officers is through an MOS transfer program, referred to as a Voluntary Lateral Move. Marine officers from other occupational specialties may apply to transfer from other specialties within the Marine Corps, such as logistics or artillery. The opportunity to transfer into CommStrat from another specialty provides both a new opportunity for the Marine and also enhances the diversity of experience and perspective within the career field.

Air Force Qualifications and Accession

As in the Navy, the Air Force PAO position requires at least a bachelor's degree, in this case in a discipline such as public relations, political science, communication, or a behavioral or social science field. The officer must be between 18 and 39 years of age and have completed Officer Training School, Reserve Officer Training Corps, or the Air Force Academy.

The Air Force accesses 25 to 35 PAOs per year. Approximately 10 to 20 percent of accessions are U.S. Air Force Academy graduates. About 70 to 80 percent come from Reserve Officer Training Corps with the remaining 10 percent from Officer Training School.

An entry-level PAO spends their time under the guidance of senior PAO, learning the technical part of the job, and learning to lead different sections of the office. The officer receives DINFOS training during this tenure if he or she has not already received it prior to this first assignment. The officer also receives on-the-job training and mentorship during this period.[18]

Officers receive the qualified level 35P3 Air Force Specialty Code following completion of the DINFOS Public Affairs Qualification Course, completion of all core tasks in the Career Field Education and Training Plan (CFETP), and 18 months of commissioned experience in a public affairs assignment.[19]

The Air Force places emphasis on professional development. With respect to public affairs, this means:

- Diversity of assignments, which may include wing, combat camera, numbered Air Force, major command, Air Staff, field operating agency/direct reporting unit, or joint public affairs positions as well as career-broadening opportunities such as squadron commander, instructor or training flight commander, political-military affairs/foreign area officer, education with industry, and so on.
- Professional military education, a relevant advanced academic degree, and supplemental DINFOS courses.
- Deploying to combat/contingency operations and participating in military exercises. Deployments and exercises are essential components of professional development; many of these opportunities are available to civilian volunteers.
- Mentorship by commanders, supervisors, and senior Air Force leaders inside and outside of the career field.

The following career planning diagram (Figure 14.4) graphically displays the types of opportunities available at different times in an Air Force PAO's career.[20]

Coast Guard Qualifications and Accession

Coast Guard Public Affairs is the smallest communication specialty of the public affairs communities discussed in this text. It is also responsible for a combination of military and law enforcement missions, complicating the execution of public affairs to a greater degree than the other services.

There are approximately 75 enlisted active-duty Coast Guard public affairs specialists, 15 full-time public affairs officers stationed in major media markets in cities around the country and collateral-duty public affairs officers, one of whom can be found at every major Coast Guard unit.[21] For commissioned officers, public affairs is not a primary career track and is considered a subspecialty that offers both junior and senior positions within the service.

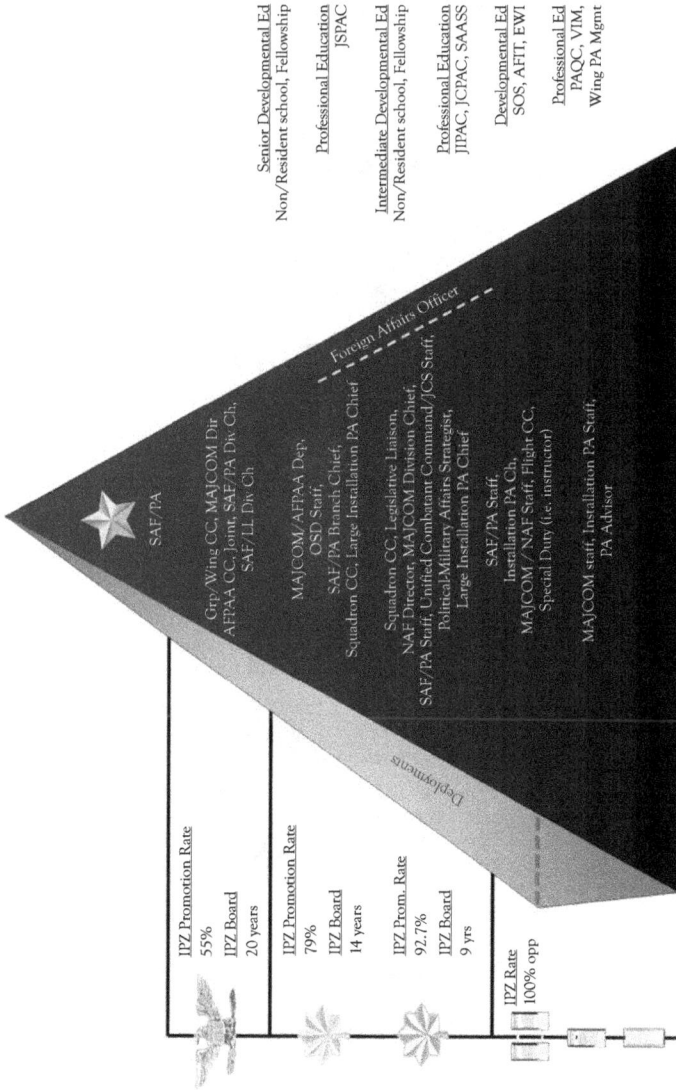

Figure 14.4 Air Force PAO Career Planning Diagram

Source: Public Domain, https://static.e-publishing.af.mil/production/1/saf_pa/publication/cfetp35p/cfetp35p.pdf

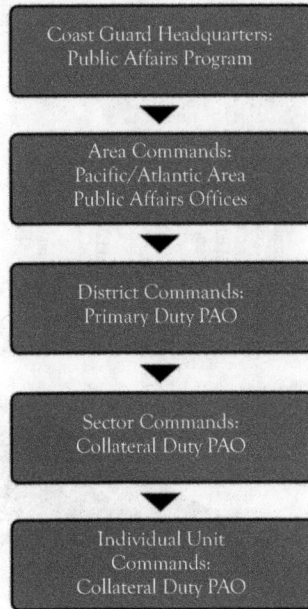

Figure 14.5 CG Public Affairs Chain of Command

Source: CDR Matt Kroll.

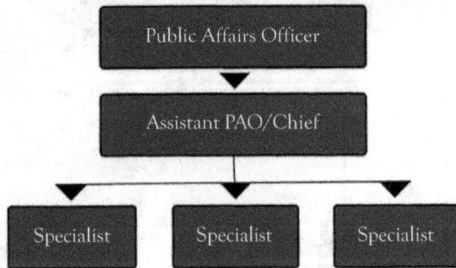

Figure 14.6 Structure of Typical CG Public Affairs Office

Source: CDR Matt Kroll.

The Office of Public Affairs includes four divisions of Media Relations, Strategic Communications, Digital Media, and Organizational Communications, in addition to a Programs Manager.[22] Regional offices operate in the Pacific and Atlantic Areas, nine districts, and at 10 public affairs detachments. In addition, multiple training commands and special Headquarters offices staff full-time public affairs personnel.[23]

Figure 14.5 shows the Coast Guard public affairs chain of command and Figure 14.6 shows the structure of the typical public affairs office.

Summary

This chapter provided insights into the qualifications and accession criteria for selection into each service's public affairs specialty. We looked at the various avenues of entry into the profession service by service. We also explored the expected competencies and career progression for each service's PAOs. While not excessively detailed, we hope this chapter provides additional insights by which the commander can assess and manage the PAOs who serve them.

CHAPTER 15

Public Affairs Employment

As described in *Joint Publication 3-61* and throughout the course of this book, public affairs officers (PAOs) carry out many roles in support of coordinated and synchronized communication. In order to do this effectively, PAOs are based or deployed in myriad locations. While all PAOs are likely to carry out the responsibilities of internal communication, external communication, media relations, and community relations, each assignment features a unique balance.

For example, each military base typically has an assigned PAO whose responsibilities focus more heavily on internal communication with the base population and community relations with those who live and support the military and local population beyond the gate. While these posts may sometimes have more predictability given the cyclic nature of on-base events like an annual 4th of July parade or quarterly community chamber of commerce meetings, they also must be prepared for crisis communication ranging from quickly informing residents and employees of military base gate closures as a result of inclement weather to ensuring safety and effective communication during an emergency, such as the COVID-19 pandemic or base evacuations due to hurricanes or wildfires.

Most deployed units also have a PAO. These PAOs may be responsible for media relations, sometimes in a combat zone. For example, the PAO would ensure media are credentialed and able to travel into the country with appropriate visas and access the military installation overseas. They also would ensure that media are able to embed with local units—including for combat operations—and must work with various news outlets or the unit with whom the embed is taking place to ensure the journalists have the protective equipment needed to carry out operations alongside the unit, such as going out on patrol beyond the security of the gate or riding in an aircraft.

Deployments and bases present several publics with whom the PAO may need to collaborate, including those that may abide by additional sets of rules and regulations. For example, overseas bases need to work closely with the local government, a different challenge than it may be stateside and that introduces a different complexity to relationships. During a deployment, a PAO may be working with multiple other military branches—known as operating in a joint environment—or with other countries, known as a combined operation, exercise, or deployment.

In addition to supporting base and overseas operations, PAOs are an integral part of services' recruiting and marketing efforts. Each service within the Department of Defense has a public affairs office within the Pentagon that provides public affairs support to the most senior leadership and also leads the service's communication efforts. Most services also have both a Los Angeles- and New York-based office that supports major news outlets and entertainment media. The entertainment media offices exist to portray the services with authenticity in order to better tell their story (see Chapter 11 for more on this subject).

For example, for productions approved by the Department of Defense that meet specific criteria for support, the Marine Corps' Entertainment Media Office helps producers, writers, and directors of nongovernment, entertainment, and nonentertainment-based media productions with the following:

- Coordination for the use of personnel, aircraft, and equipment.
- Access to Marine Corps installations, both within the United States and forward combat zones.
- Assistance in obtaining broadcast-quality Marine Corps stock footage and "B" roll footage.
- Accurate script and story development.
- Access to highly qualified subject matter experts (i.e., pilots, engineers, infantrymen, and so on.)[1]

The services' Aerial Demonstration Teams, including the Navy's Blue Angels and the Air Force's Thunderbirds, also have a PAO who leads the team's extensive marketing, publicity, and community relations programs but also must be equally equipped for media relations and crisis communications.

In any situation, a PAO is expected to serve as an effective communicator and strategic thinker. They must have strong relationships with higher headquarters, adjacent units, and community leadership to make sure they can support as needed, and they must understand and be integrated into the unit's mission in order to develop and execute plans that employ a balance of the skills described at the beginning of this section.

PART V

The Future of Military Public Affairs

This part explores possible future trends in public affairs, as mirrored in predictions for the civilian practice of public relations. While it is impossible to say with certainty that these trends will continue or that new trends might not take their place, the authors suggest these are the most likely trends that should be considered going forward.

CHAPTER 16

The Way Forward

If we fail to adapt, we fail to move forward.

—John Wooden[1]

The central thesis of this book is that public affairs and the art and science of effective communications have never been more important and that military public affairs more closely mirrors the civilian practice than ever before. A subset of that thesis is that the way forward for both civilian and military practice is rooted in adaptation. This chapter addresses a few of the top trends for the future of public relations and the implications of these trends for the practice of military public affairs.

Trust, Purpose, and Reputation

Layered data-driven decision making is paramount in building or sustaining communication outcomes such as trust, clear purpose, and reputation. To support national and global security with communications efforts that demonstrate authenticity, the military PAO's skills and strategic foresight must continue to evolve, especially with emerging virtual communication landscapes from which opinions and sentiment can be shaped. Along with those skills and foresight, the PAO must be able to represent a path to these qualitative outcomes with quantitative data, which will be discussed later in this chapter. This requires a deeper knowledge of data analysis and an increased cadence or re-structure of output, coupled with consistent credibility and compelling storytelling.

Big Data

The concept of *Big Data* has been around for at least the last decade and the debate on how to use it in a strategic communications setting is still in its infancy. Weiner and Kochhar (2016) define *Big Data* as "advanced technology that allows large volumes of data to drive more fully integrated decision-making."[2] In other words, *Big Data* "is larger, more complex data sets from a wide array of sources."[3] Civilian public relations professionals focus mainly on the benefits of *Big Data* in terms of finding and appealing to consumers. Military PAOs have a number of ways to advantage *Big Data* beyond this focus.

For one, *Big Data* can be used in conjunction with social listening to understand sentiment, or the views or attitudes of stakeholders. This helps create messaging that more perfectly aligns with stakeholder values, making communication efforts more effective and efficient. Military public affairs typically suffers from constrained budgets, so anything that improves effectiveness and efficiency is most welcome.

Similarly, PAOs can use *Big Data* for "landscape analysis," as Weiner and Kochhar (2016) label it, or situational awareness (SA) in the military parlance. Typically, SA includes a competitive analysis of the internal and external operating environment, including what public relations efforts exist and media trend analysis, to make better communications decisions. *Big Data* can broaden the scope of the SA to include additional data points such as societal trends that help the PAO better align organizational and stakeholder priorities and know better where to focus time and energy.

Arguably, the most important part of any strategic plan is its objectives. As discussed in Chapter 7, it is essential that objectives should be measurable, meaningful, attainable, and reasonable for the plan to be successful. *Big Data* can uncover valuable insights for the PAO that aid with more robust objective determination.

Likewise, strategy and tactic development can be improved with the use of *Big Data*. Instead of relying on a "seat-of-the-pants" approach, the PAO can utilize the insights from analyzing these data sets to achieve more accurate and effective targeting of strategies and tactics. *Big Data* analysis also enables PAOs to see what operational elements outside of public affairs may be affected and to what degree through different public affairs results.

Finally, *Big Data* allows for improved and more robust evaluation of the strategic campaign plan. PAOs have traditionally relied on media analysis and insights gained from focus groups and survey (if they were lucky and had the time and resources) to evaluate campaign success. With *Big Data*, the number of factors to be considered in such an evaluation exponentially expands, allowing the PAO to better articulate the impact of their efforts to the Commander and senior staff.

Artificial Intelligence

Closely related to *Big Data* is the use of Artificial Intelligence, or AI. PAOs can use AI to send direct, relevant messages to specific audiences, as "real-time big data offers practitioners the information they need to provide current content that consumers want to see."[4]

With its ability to process human language, AI can help PAOs better understand individual behaviors, preference, beliefs, and interest. This knowledge helps them deliver more efficient campaign strategies.[5]

Mainstream media outlets such as *The Washington Post, Bloomberg,* and the *BBC* are currently using AI to write stories. According to a 2021 study by the Knight Foundation, the primary use of AI in journalism today was for "augmenting reporting capacity."[6] According to their report, these media outlets use AI to "comb through large document dumps with machine learning, detect breaking news events in social media, and scrape COVID-19 data from government websites."[7] It is logical to assume that PAOs can also use this technology to likewise improve their communication capabilities.

Perhaps one of the most impactful uses of AI is in capturing and mitigating bad news. Scholars are already developing the protocols that would be used in the machine learning process required to build predictive models on both the severity of a crisis and the appropriate response. Given the amount of time PAOs spend responding to crises and media inquiries, this capability could be a game changer.

Diversification of the Public Affairs Domain

As previously discussed, new platforms continue to arise with startlingly rapidity. PAOs need to quickly understand these new platforms and their appropriateness for the task at hand.

A key factor in this adaptation effort is the growing need to leverage multimedia content in communicating with stakeholders and understanding how to do so. Research shows that video enhances both accessibility to and engagement with messages, especially on social media.[8] While creating multimedia content is typically the responsibility of the public affairs staff, PAOs need to completely understand the process. The curriculum at DINFOS contains some exposure to multimedia content but this is an appropriate area for expanding professional development going forward.

Virtual/Augmented Reality

Virtual reality (VR) and augmented reality (AR) created a great deal of excitement when they first hit the scene as commercially viable entities, especially within the advertising and marketing industries. While they have yet to live up to their promise, there are nonetheless potential uses for military public affairs, two of which are discussed here.

Among the current uses of VR/AR is creating an immersive experience from static objects. This lends itself well to use in a variety of community relations activities. AR could add value to static displays at air shows and open houses by providing additional details about the display through a click on one's smart phone.

VR/AR can create opportunities for journalists, influencers, and legislators to experience the military without having to coordinate a physical visit or trip. The technology offers new and immersive ways that allow PAOs to bypass traditional media familiarization trips, lessening the impact of such trips on both the PAO and his or her staff and the operational commands being showcased. The facilities, people, and operations can come alive with a modicum of up-front preparation and production.

Roles and Responsibilities

Since their humble beginnings in the military, the PAO has constantly fought for a voice at the decision-making table so they can include effective theory-based communication strategies, objectives, and best practices in the operational plan. As mentioned throughout this book, the PAO's role grows increasingly more important in both the advisory role and as a professional.

As an adviser, the PAO must help senior leaders navigate through the media environment by knowing the landscape and predicting possible outcomes. PAOs also need to monitor trends in real-time, find various stakeholder touchpoints through social listening, and offer predictive analysis. They then need to integrate these insights into their strategic communication planning and advice to the commander.

In terms of the practice of military public affairs, what mattered to stakeholders three years ago looks incredibly different today. This requires the PAO to know how certain tactics and strategies may resonate with stakeholders at any given time.[9] It also requires the PAO to adapt to new technology to ensure the military's limited public relations resources are effectively and efficiently deployed to uphold national and global security. This particular point will be discussed in more depth later in this chapter.

Public Affairs Must Be Part of the Larger Ecosystem

PAOs have made steady progress earning a voice on the decision-making team. A key to continuing this integration is the PAO being a productive part of the larger ecosystem. Transparency and engagement with other players on the staff are the pathway to success in this endeavor.

Solid, positive relationships rely on two-way communication and a *quid pro quo* approach. Knowing where relevant information resides and retrieving that information when needed is only part of the battle. Keeping the PAO's network humming with information useful to those sources creates the kind of collaborative environment where everyone thrives and succeeds.

PAOs frequently know things before the operational side of the command does. Though the adage "information is power" may have merit in some circles, it can be death in the public affairs arena so PAOs need to freely offer what they know in these instances to enable rapid coordination and rectification of the problem. Especially when crises hit, holding one's cards close to the chest is a recipe for compounding the problem, including greater hits to the reputation of the organization.

Future Training: Formal Education

Formal education for the PAO has evolved from the informal "on-the-job" training of the 1930s and 1940s, to the creation of military-specific training centers for officers and enlisted members in the 1950s and 1960s, to a heavy reliance on academic courses at civilian colleges and universities in the 1970s and 1980s. Today, the military uses all three training methods to provide a well-rounded knowledge base for their professional PAOs.

One way to continue to develop the field of military public relations is to strengthen the partnership between the military and civilian colleges and universities. Although some scientific studies exist that focus on military and government communications, an abundance of opportunities still exist for scholars and professionals to explore the unique characteristics of military public relations. The results of such studies will benefit the military PAO and the larger body of knowledge in public relations.

"Upskilling:" The Importance of Professional Development, Qualifications, and Life-Long Learning

The communication landscape changes at such a rapid pace that the skills PAOs acquire in training are already starting to be dated when they enter the field. To keep pace with the industry and to continue to effectively perform as counselors and professionals, the military needs to embrace the importance of professional development qualifications more rapidly, such as PR accreditation and ongoing "upskilling" for the public affairs community.

Providing PAOs with professional development opportunities like those that their civilian counterparts enjoy ensures that the PAO's knowledge and skills stay relevant and up-to-date and that they are aware of changing trends and directions in the industry.

Additionally, encouraging military PAOs to earn their PR accreditation (APR+M) through the Public Relations Society of America (PRSA) boosts their credibility both with their commanders and civilian counterparts and helps to build partnerships between the military, academia, and the civilian public relations industry.

Advanced degrees have always been important for officers to improve their chances at promotion. They are becoming critical for military PAOs as the need for a more strategic approach to communication becomes increasingly important. Rear Admiral Terry L. "T" McCreary saw the need for this in the early 2000s when he negotiated a partnership between the Navy and San Diego State University for a 10-month "PAO Program" leading to a Master's in Mass Communication and Media Studies. As discussed in Chapter 13, the Army and Navy have a partnership with Georgetown University and the Air Force has an Education with Industry program. Each seeks to help military PAOs be more strategic in their planning, coordination, and execution of communication plans.

The 2017 Commission on Public Relations Education "Report on Undergraduate Education" noted the following skills an entry-level practitioner should have, based on a survey of public relations professionals in either an agency or corporate setting with hiring authority:[10]

- Research and analytics
- Writing
- Media relations
- Social media management
- Editing
- Public speaking
- Storytelling
- Communication

Most professionals and educators agree that these skills are still relevant, despite the age of this report.

A more recent blog discussion on the "7 Must-Have Public Relations Skills" by *Muck Rack*[11] hits another set of skills that are absolutely essential for the military PAO. Although intended to equip the civilian public relations professional, each skill set presented could easily have been written with the military PAO in mind. They are:

- *Attention to detail*—In public affairs, as in the rest of the military, details are crucial.

- *Ability to roll with the punches*—Thick skin is crucial in public affairs as PAOs generally hear more about the ones they lose than the ones they win.
- *Quick thinking*—Deadlines, strategy, and demands are constantly changing in public relations so the ability to think on your feet is crucial to mission success.
- *Creativity*—Innovative ideas and messages that are well thought out are essential to break through the clutter in communication.
- *Relationship Building*—Public affairs is all about relationships; knowing where information resides within the command and building a rapport with those sources is key to developing, coordinating, and executing effective strategic communication campaigns.
- *Staying up to date on news and trends*—PAOs are expected to have their fingers on the pulse of the command, the community, indeed, the world.
- *Strong writing skills*—"Although content takes many shapes these days, the fundamental rules of writing stay the same: No matter the medium, convey your story or idea briefly, accurately, creatively, articulately and grammatically correct (Even if it's a 280-character tweet)."[12]

New Media

Limited by policy that struggles to keep pace with new and emerging media, the military PAO must balance being adaptable and facile with this ever-changing communication toolkit with the knowledge of how to employ public relations theories as the basis for communications planning. Tactics will continue to change over time as new technologies emerge. The competent PAO must continue to think beyond the immediate tasks of creating content for these new media and, instead, continue to develop strategic and long-term communications objectives that transcend existing and emerging media.

One of the more recent developments in this pursuit is the PESO Model™. As Gini Diedrich explains in her *SpinSucks* blog post, "The

PESO Model takes the four media types—paid, earned, shared, and owned—and merges them together" [13] (see Figure 16.1).

Military PAOs can use the PESO framework as a strategic tool to understand the relationship between media and tactics as part of an integrated strategic communication campaign. When used as part of that plan, PESO provides a menu of media options with each format aligned to a variety of objectives and outcomes.[14] The model helps the PAO understand and enhance the strengths and weaknesses of various media types, which in turn helps build reputation, credibility, trust, thought leadership, and authority. The model is most valuable to PAOs when they properly analyze the areas of overlap between forms of media and the opportunity for amplification, promotion, and third-party validation.[15]

Measurement and Evaluation

Military PAOs need to continue to push for resources and time for research and planning at the beginning of campaigns or PR programs, measurement throughout execution of the campaign, and evaluation at the end to gain insights into the effectiveness of their efforts in meeting the commander's intent and his or her goals and objectives. The focus needs to shift from *output-level* metrics such as impressions, reach, or "hits" to measuring *outcomes* including reputation, relationship, and trust building and advocacy.

This will require military PAOs to be better trained in data analytics and to have access to industry-standard tools, such as Google Analytics, Cision, and the International Association for Measurement and Evaluation of Communication (AMEC) Integrated Evaluation Framework tool.

Measurement and evaluation remain a central concern for public relations professionals, which should include military PAOs. It is not the purpose of this chapter to go into detail on how to accomplish these tasks but to highlight its importance for PAOs going forward. For more on the topic, a very through and excellent explanation of public relations research and measurement, including campaign evaluation, is contained in *A Practitioner's Guide to Public Relations Research, Measurement, and Evaluation*, another of the Public Relations Collection works by Don Stacks and David Michaelson.[16]

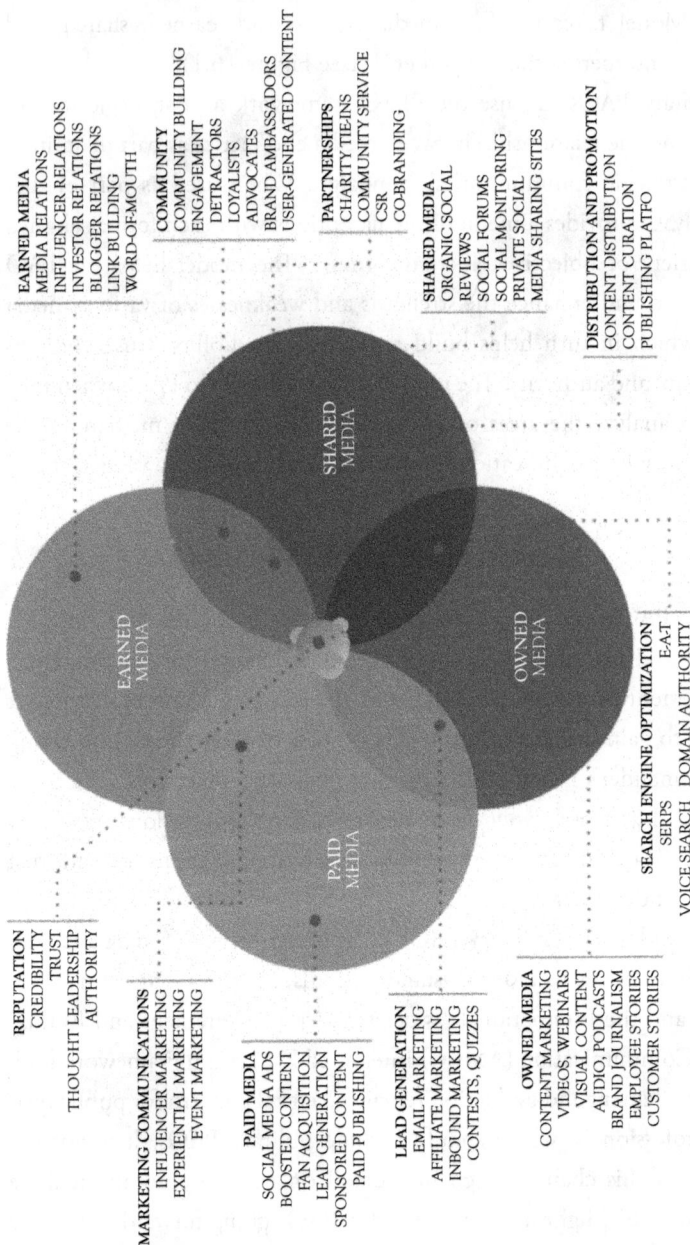

Figure 16.1 The Peso Model

(*Used with permission*)

Live Events

Live events have been an integral part of the public relations toolkit since the early days of the profession. What was once deemed a publicity stunt or pseudo-event, progressed into operational demonstrations, news briefings, and many other public events used by the military today. There is an inherent value in having reporters, and the public, see and experience events with their own eyes. The first-person account adds a layer of authenticity that is very difficult to achieve with the standard release of an information subsidy (news release, fact sheet, brochure, etc.).

Over the past few years, we have seen live events include a virtual attendance element, as "live" events were canceled during the pandemic. Moving forward, we should expect to see the virtual element remain because it adds convenience for the military and the media and as discussed earlier who are often both restricted by time and resources.

The challenge with any virtual element is providing an experience that is comparable to that which those who are attending the event in person receive. Two key variables to help achieve this equilibrium for live events are the visuals and information content.

The first key variable is the quality and variety of the imagery that is available to virtual attendees. Defense Media Activity (DMA) production teams provide professional video broadcast services for high-profile events, complete with multiple video cameras and a mobile, live-broadcast production trailer. This professional-quality service will ensure stakeholders see a variety of aspects of the event, but these resources are extremely limited. The only other option, aside from using DMA, is to have the local public affairs staff use a third-party video streaming service such as going "live" on social media or using a web-based video conference service, such as Zoom or Microsoft Teams.

In the future, we can expect to see the technical gap between these two options close as web-based services continue to meet the demand for higher production value video products. Military commanders need to make sure their public affairs staff is trained for this increased demand and has the equipment needed to produce the highest quality product. This is especially important for visually driven events, such as operational demonstrations, fleet weeks, and open houses.

For information-based live events, such as news briefings, ceremonies, and major announcements, great attention must be given to the content, style, and timing of the message. These are the elements the virtual audience uses to fill the voids caused by the lack of nonverbal communication cues.[17] In-person attendees benefit from these nonverbal cues to deepen their understanding of the information being provided. Just as information is adapted for different media (i.e., formal news release vs. social media), we must acknowledge that there are two separate audiences who are receiving information through different means at the same event.

A basic example of this approach is a professional sporting event. There are clear elements in place that cater to the in-person attendees and others for the TV viewers, giving the audience a choice of two different ways to experience the live event. As long as the military continues to embrace this dual-audience approach by improving the visual elements to meet the growing expectations of the public and crafting information to specifically engage the virtual audience, live events will continue to be an effective public relations tool for the military to impart knowledge, build trust, and establish positive relationships with our stakeholders.

Seizing the Opportunity

In this final section, we offer some general thoughts on the future of trust in our society. Though not front-and-center in this endeavor, the military can nonetheless assist in this process. Our focus here, however, is on the opportunities for society to manage the pace of change, respond to change, and determine how information is protected and revealed.

As the pandemic continued to surge, hope that institutions would rise to the moment and show leadership faded. Just more than two years after COVID-19 took over, trust is bankrupt. Recent events including protests against the 2020 election outcome, violence at the U.S. Capitol, and brazen lawlessness have taken a heavy toll on trust. Restoring trust is not going to be easy and may end up requiring rebuilding completely, from the ground up. Our expectations should be high.

Trust in business is growing as tech companies are limiting access to their platforms for people, organizations, and bots that spread mis- or mal-information or who disagree with their narrative. We can re-establish trust in the media by holding information sources and news outlets accountable. Trust in government and NGOs can be rebuilt with what the Edelman Trust Barometer describes as leading with facts and empathy. But it is a steep road ahead.

Improving Education

Rebuilding trust means reinvigorating civics education at all levels and for all ages, and this requirement goes beyond a basic education in how governments function to include the skills necessary to participate in civil society. The military can lead the way here.

Everyone, especially the troops, needs to know how to analyze news and communication for dis-information, mis-information, and mal-information, determine truth in public discourse, and assess the impact of individual as well as organizational responsibilities for maintaining standards of truth. Absent this critical thinking and the ability to discern the difference between facts and mis- or mal-information, the resulting vacuum creates a culture ripe for the growth of lies, conspiracy theories, and "alternative facts."

The Department of Defense is seeing the efficacy of this approach as it has shared pages from the Russian playbook and select intelligence information to inoculate the public against Russian dis-, mis-, and mal-information in the Ukraine war. As mentioned earlier, the Public Relations Society of America has an ongoing effort to raise awareness about and combat mis-information/dis-information.[18]

In addition, education must continue beyond formal schooling. Tech companies should help users to determine the truthfulness of available information, continue to monitor social media platforms, establish processes enabling users to learn how to avoid hackers, and recognize scams and sites with ill intent. Military public affairs must support and amplify these initiatives. And both parties must do this all without violating individual rights to free speech and privacy.

Focusing on Change

Other changes in public confidence in institutions have taken center stage as revealed by the results of the 2020 Edelman poll. This shift in confidence in institutions was highlighted by the public's growing trust in the government to provide information about the pandemic. According to Edelman, trust in government sources surged 11 percent, with the public relying on government for protection at a level of trust not seen since World War II. In 2020, respondents wanted the government to continue to provide economic relief (86 percent), to get the country back to normal (79 percent), to contain the spread of the virus (73 percent), and to keep the public informed (86 percent). By the end of 2020, when these things failed to materialize, trust tanked again.

There are growing expectations for the business sector to partner with government in improving the economy and building new job opportunities. This expectation represents an inflection point for both businesses and NGOs, going beyond corporate social responsibility. Never has the need been greater for collaborative and cooperative approaches to rebuilding not only the economy, but also the underpinnings of society— education, access to health care, opportunities for fair housing, a boost to the minimum wage, and the potential for living a full life.

While the May 2020 study revealed the pandemic has turned many trust variables on their head, the need for fair and accurate media coverage remains a critical point. Trust in traditional media grew seven points from January to May 2020, but by January 2021 that fragile trust bubble had burst. The stated trust in government to provide timely, factual information about the pandemic, to support to the economy, and to help struggling families proved more aspirational than realistic. The latest Edelman survey revealed trust in all information sources has hit a new low, reaching 35 percent for social media and only 58 percent for traditional media.

Social media platforms are likewise beginning to take stronger action to moderate content and prevent users from breaking the law. In the aftermath of the riot at the U.S. Capitol on January 6, 2021, big tech began to take action regarding the use of their platforms. Twitter closed former President Trump's account and others began to take action to stop mis-information from spreading. These efforts may be cynically viewed as an attempt to stave off government regulation of tech, but they represent the beginning of a change in how platforms view responsibility for how their products are used. Critics claim these actions are undemocratic and violate the First Amendment. It is important that we watch this debate and these actions closely in the future.

While many individuals continue to practice what Edelman terms "poor information hygiene"—not checking sources and blithely passing on mis-information—others are increasingly unwilling to merely accept information as it is delivered. Yet this approach comes with a couple of cautions: beware of confirmation bias and seeking only that which matches your previously held beliefs.

Many now question sources, demand transparency, and explore references and sources. One would expect this to bode well for journalism—greater public involvement should mean more thorough fact checking and increased awareness of scams, falsehoods, and hacks. There are more sites that support determining truth in news, both in terms of ferreting out manipulated media—from photographs to videos—and in determining false sources, lies, and bias. These range from Ad Fontes Media's bell curve of bias in news to a number of nonpartisan, fact-checking sites such as listed on Middlebury Libraries homepage. The PAO must be able to continually be mindful of these problems and continually prepared to counter such reports both within and outside the military.

As fallout from political mayhem and pandemic of 2020 and 2021 continues to push democratic institutions to move beyond the Information Apocalypse, a number of efforts will become more prevalent and visible; PAOs must not only observe but take into account how these will impact their services and their messaging strategy and practices:

- Increasing focus on stricter terms of service and regulation of tech firms, antitrust cases, and a major focus on corporate responsibility for safeguarding privacy and truth.
- New respect for the planet, environmental safeguards, awareness of the effects of global warming, and the creative abilities of science.
- Increased partnering by state governments and business to protect privacy, stop hackers, find and force out bots and trolls, delete false accounts, and call out those who incite violence.

- Growing transparency in intelligence and awareness that shared information can effectively prevent false narratives and influence campaigns.

These actions represent the signs of a coming transformation, a culture shift from the Information Age's "apocalyptic Wild West" to tomorrow's "Knowledge Age." In this next information era, *trust will be paramount*. The responsibility for creating this massive cultural change lies with everyone: military, governments, businesses, nongovernmental organizations, and the media—in short with all institutions that have a stake in preserving trust and truth—and with all citizens.

Thankfully, a harsh and dystopian future is not guaranteed. We need to consciously develop media literacy standards in education at all levels, mandate responsible media, and build public trust and confidence in the knowledge that the false will be found out and eliminated.

These transformative actions are significant in and of themselves, but it is critical to go further. According to futurist Anne Lise Kjaer, "Things no longer change over a generation or a decade, but from year to year, even month to month, creating new arenas for disruptive ideas and innovation to emerge … Inevitably, this leads us to reconsider the future and our place within it." PAOs must act in order to make sense of the rapid pace of change, today, and tomorrow, developing not just civics or media literacy but also "futures literacy," the capacity to know how and why to imagine the future.[19]

Many organizations are going even further, determined to meet future challenges head on. Businesses are scheduling foresight sessions, hosted by futurist companies like the Institute for the Future. The Institute and similar organizations train business and government organizations to identify disruptors, recognize trends, develop opportunities for change management, and scout out indications of emerging possibilities. Today's volatile operating environment has leaders realizing the key to prevailing in an uncertain future lies in the ability to not only identify potential change but also to adapt in advance. A major factor in the ability to adapt is the willingness to partner, for institutions to work together and lead with facts and empathy.

But at the most basic level, responsibility for this change begins with the individual. Citizens must take measures to secure and protect their privacy online and in the public space. Education must become more robust and available at all levels, not just in schools. Leaders must drive change within their organizations and cultures. While many experts predict digital life in the future will improve, they also caution that people must be engaged in the process to effect this transformation. Foresight increases agility and the ability to adapt and ensures that the fears many hold today are fully addressed. Basic rights and economic fairness must be taken into account and watched carefully.

With effort, tomorrow's social media platforms will be increasingly responsible and committed to protecting the privacy and rights of its users. Future citizens will undoubtedly be better informed because they can have trust and confidence in the knowledge they possess, know their privacy is secure, and can trust their institutions. The Knowledge Age is there to be created, shaped, and developed by today's tech firms, policy experts, and citizen activists. Everyone must embrace these innovations and reforms, insist on basic rights and fairness, and demand factual information that we can all trust, rely upon, and use with confidence.

At the beginning of this chapter, we stated that the way forward for both civilian and military public affairs (public relations) professionals is rooted in adaptation. While no one has a functioning crystal ball, we have outlined here a few of the top trends for the future of public relations and the implications of these trends for the practice of military public affairs. In every case, the PAO will need to add the ability to acclimatize to the nature and pace of change, respond to and manage that change, and determine how to best use the advancements in the profession.

Notes

Preface

1. Public Relations Society of America (PRSA) (n.d.).

Chapter 1

1. PRSA (n.d.a).
2. Ibid.
3. Ibid.
4. Wikipedia (n.d.a).
5. U.S. Army (n.d.a).
6. "What is Public Affairs" (n.d.).
7. Kirby (2000).
8. PRSA (n.d.b).
9. *Today's Military* (n.d.a).
10. PRSA, op. cit.
11. Today's Military (n.d.b).

Chapter 2

1. Douglas (2002).
2. Ibid.
3. Ibid.
4. Aukofer and Lawrence (1995), p. 35.
5. Nelson (1967), pp. 229–230.
6. Stephens (1978), p.19.
7. Library of Congress (n.d.).
8. Brown (1967), p. 389.
9. The Reporters Committee for Freedom of the Press (n.d.).
10. Dennis (1992), p. 10.

11. Mock (1941), p. 103.
12. Aukofer and Lawrence, op. cit., pp. 38–39.
13. Ibid.
14. Ibid.
15. Lamay, FitzSimon, and Sahadi (1991), p. 11.
16. Ibid.
17. Aukofer and Lawrence, op.cit., p. 39.
18. Ibid.
19. Ibid, p. 40.
20. Venable (2002), p. 67.
21. Lamay, et. al., op. cit., p. 39.
22. Ibid.
23. Aukofer and Lawrence, op. cit., p. 44.
24. Ibid.
25. Ibid, p. 45.
26. Ibid.
27. Nathanman (1999).
28. Grantham (2000).
29. Wright (2004), p. S-1.
30. Ibid, p. S-2.
31. Bereiter (2016).
32. Stephen (2022).
33. Kurtz (n.d.).

Chapter 3

1. Department of Defense (2017).
2. Ibid.
3. Ibid.
4. Ibid.
5. Department of Defense (2014).
6. Washington Headquarters Service (n.d.).
7. Universal Accreditation Board (2017).
8. Department of Defense (2007).
9. Department of Defense (1993).
10. White and Dozier (1992).

11. Ibid.
12. Neill and Drumwright (2012), pp. 220–234.
13. Ibid, p. 224.
14. PRSA (n.d.c).
15. Ibid.
16. Ibid.
17. Universal Accreditation Board, op. cit.
18. Ibid.
19. Ibid.
20. PRSA (2021).

Chapter 4

1. Ocalya (@metaviv) (2018).
2. Gallup. Inc. (n.d.).
3. Shane (2019).
4. Schudson (2019).
5. American Historical Association (n.d.).
6. Public Broadcast System (n.d.).
7. New York Times (n.d.).
8. Panja (2019).
9. Baer (2019).
10. Seifert (2020).
11. Carvajal (n.d.).
12. Spector (2020).
13. Cassidy (2019).
14. Ransom (2020).
15. Josephson (2005).
16. Fox (2017).
17. Brittain and Carmon (2018).
18. Hubbard (2021).
19. Ungarino (2019).
20. Tapper (2016).
21. Corn (2020).
22. Rogan (2013).
23. Bethal College (2021).

24. Noor (2020).

25. Ad Fontes Media (n.d.).

26. Wikipedia (n.d.b).

27. Mueller (2019).

28. Atlantic Council (2019).

29. Moshin (2021).

30. Shearer and Matsa (2018).

31. Ma and Gilbert (2019).

32. Tech Republic Staff (2020).

33. GDPR.EU (n.d.).

34. Browne (2020).

35. Edelman (2018).

36. Ibid.

37. Wallace (2016).

38. Wall Street Journal Editorial Board (2022).

39. Quell (2020).

40. Wiseman (2015).

41. Ibid.

42. Burns, Laskowski, and Tucci (n.d.).

43. Westerheide (2020).

44. Edelman, op. cit.

45. Brenan (2021).

46. Mitchell, Grieco, and Sumida (n.d.).

47. Middlebury Libraries (2021).

48. American University (2021).

Chapter 5

1. O'Malley (1920).

2. Edelman, op. cit.

3. McCarthy (2018).

4. Greenhut (2013).

5. Abbott (1988).

6. Ibid.

7. The Media Insight Project (2018).

8. Marantz (2019).

9. McLennan and Miles (n.d.).

10. Clabaugh (2019).

11. Andrew (2020).

12. Jurkowitz, Mitchell, Santhanam, Adams, Anderson, and Vogt (2013).

13. Kazden (2017).

14. The Media Insight Project (2016).

15. Davies (2019).

16. Parker (2015).

17. Quick and Larson (2018).

18. Heshmat (2015).

19. The Young Turks, Inc. (n.d.).

20. Wikipedia (n.d.c).

21. Brown (2019).

22. Allen (2019).

23. Ibid.

24. Brown, op. cit.

25. Wikipedia (n.d.d).

26. Ajaka, Kessler, and Samuels (2019).

27. Wikipedia (n.d.).

28. Jenkins (2019).

29. Nieman Lab (n.d.e)

Chapter 6

1. Sinek (2015).

2. Yaffa (2020).

3. Panetta (2019).

4. FBI (2017).

5. New Yorker, op. cit.

6. West and Bergstrom (2017).

7. Center for an Informed Public (n.d.).

8. Simonite (2020).

9. Edelman, op. cit.

10. Thunberg (2019).

11. Rayome (2019).

12. Bowden (2020).
13. Black Lives Matter (n.d.).
14. Edelman (n.d.).
15. Jones and Lloyd (n.d.).
16. Edelman (2020).
17. Rosen, Harbath, Gleicher, and Leathern (2019).
18. Kjaer (n.d.).
19. Standsberry, Anderson, and Raine (n.d.).

Chapter 7

1. Stacks (n.d.); Michaelson and Stacks (2017).
2. Ibid, p. 24.
3. Michaelson, Wright, and Stacks (n.d.), pp. 1–25.

Chapter 8

1. Dolphin (2005), pp. 171–190.
2. Strandberg and Vigsø (2016), pp. 89–102.

Chapter 11

1. Broom and Dozier (1986), pp. 37–56.
2. Ibid.

Chapter 12

1. Broom and Sha (2013).
2. Ibid.
3. PRSA, op.cit.
4. DoD Directive 5122.0, op.cit.
5. Headquarters Marine Corps (n.d.).
6. Broom and Shaw, op.cit.
7. Ibid.
8. Department of Defense (2012).
9. Department of Defense (2016).

10. Broom and Shaw, op.cit.
11. Department of Defense (2016), op.cit.

Chapter 13

1. Defense Information School (n.d.a).
2. Defense Information School (n.d.b).
3. Ibid.
4. Defense Information School (n.d.c).
5. Defense Information School (n.d.d).
6. Ibid.
7. Defense Information School (n.d.e).
8. Defense Information School (n.d.f).
9. Defense Information School (n.d.g).
10. Ibid.
11. Ibid.
12. Defense Information School (n.d.h).
13. San Diego State University (n.d.).
14. Department of the Army (n.d.).
15. Air Force Institute of Technology (n.d.).

Chapter 14

1. Department of the Army (2010).
2. Ibid.
3. Ibid.
4. Ibid.
5. Ibid.
6. Ibid.
7. Ibid.
8. Ibid.
9. Ibid.
10. Ibid.
11. Navy Bureau of Personnel (2019).
12. Ibid.
13. Ibid.

14. Naval Personnel Command (2002).

15. Navy Bureau of Personnel (2021).

16. Chandran, DeFrancisco, Fugler, and Seasit (2002).

17. Navy Chief of Information (2020).

18. Department of the Air Force (2018).

19. Ibid.

20. Ibid.

21. Lehman (2017).

22. U.S. Coast Guard [USCG] (2021).

23. Kroll (2017).

Chapter 15

1. U.S. Marine Corps (n.d.).

Chapter 16

1. Wooden and Carter (2014).

2. Weiner and Kochhar (2016).

3. Peterson (n.d.).

4. Rogers (2019).

5. Maldanodo (2020).

6. Keefe, Zhou, and Merrill (2021).

7. Ibid.

8. Clarine (2016).

9. Keily (2022).

10. Commission on Public Relations Education (2017).

11. Burt (2021).

12. Ibid.

13. Dietrich (2022).

14. Waddington (2018).

15. Little (2020).

16. Stacks and Michaelson (2010).

17. Handke, Schulte, Schneider, and Kauffeld (2018).

18. PRSA (2022).

19. Larson, Mortenson, and Miller (2020).

References

Abbott, A. 1988. *The System of Professions: An Essay on the Division of Expert Labor*. Chicago: University of Chicago Press.

Ad Fontes Media. n.d. "Interactive Media Bias Chart." www.adfontesmedia.com/interactive-media-bias-chart/ (accessed on October 08, 2021).

Air Force Institute of Technology. n.d. "Civilian Institution Programs." www.afit.edu/CIP/page.cfm?page=1567 (accessed on August 15, 2021).

Ajaka, N., G. Kessler, and E. Samuels. 2019. "The Washington Post's Guide to Manipulated Video." Washington Post. www.washingtonpost.com/graphics/2019/politics/fact-checker/manipulated-video-guide/ (accessed on October 08, 2021).

Allen, M. 2019. "Zuckerberg Wants Facebook's News Tab to Do 'a Better Job of Supporting Journalism.'" Axios. www.axios.com/facebook-news-tab-mark-zuckerberg-interview-4935b1d4-25ed-4856-981e-e9b3b2e4551e.html (accessed on October 08, 2021).

American Historical Association. n.d. "The Story of Propaganda." www.historians.org/about-aha-and-membership/aha-history-and-archives/gi-roundtable-series/pamphlets/em-2-what-is-propaganda-(1944)/the-story-of-propaganda (accessed on October 08, 2021).

American University. 2021. "What Are Reliable Sources for Fact-Checking and Recognizing 'Fake News'?" American University Library. https://answers.library.american.edu/faq/282165 (accessed on October 08, 2021).

Andrew, S. 2020. "There's a Growing Call to Defund the Police. Here's What Is Means." CNN. www.cnn.com/2020/06/06/us/what-is-defund-police-trnd/index.html (accessed on October 08, 2021).

Atlantic Council. 2019. "US National Security Advisor LTG H.R. McMaster: Russian Aggression Is Strengthening Our Resolve." Atlantic Council. www.atlanticcouncil.org/commentary/transcript/us-national-security-advisor-lt-gen-h-r-mcmaster-russian-aggression-is-strengthening-our-resolve/ (accessed on October 08, 2021).

Aukofer, F. and W.P. Lawrence. 1995. *America's Team: The odd couple*, P. 35. Nashville: The Freedom Forum First Amendment Center.

Baer, B. 2019. "Video: Astros Relay Signs to Hitters by Banging on a Trash Can in 2017." NBC Sports. https://mlb.nbcsports.com/2019/11/12/video-astros-relay-signs-to-hitters-by-banging-on-a-trash-can-in-2017/ (accessed on October 08, 2021).

Bereiter, G. 2016. "The U.S. Navy in Operation Enduring Freedom, 2001–2002." Washington Navy Yard, D.C.: Navy History and Heritage Center. www.history.navy.mil/research/library/online-reading-room/title-list-alphabetically/u/us-navy-operation-enduring-freedom-2001-2002.html. (accessed on May 23, 2022).

Bethal College. 2021. "Fake News or Real? or How to Become Media Savvy: Confirmation Bias." Bethal College Library Guides. https://bethelks.libguides.com/c.php?g=591268&p=4194631 (accessed on October 08, 2021).

Black Lives Matter. n.d. "About." https://blacklivesmatter.com/about/ (accessed on October 08, 2021).

Bowden, J. 2020. "Tim Cook Praises Supreme Court Ruling on DACA." The Hill. https://thehill.com/policy/technology/tech-execs/503382-tim-cook-praises-supreme-court-ruling-on-daca (accessed on October 08, 2021).

Brenan, M. 2021. "America's Trust in Media Dips to Second Lowest on Record." Gallup. https://news.gallup.com/poll/355526/americans-trust-media-dips-second-lowest-record.aspx. (accessed on October 08, 2021).

Brittain, A. and I. Carmon. 2018. "Charlie Rose's Misconduct Was Widespread at CBS and Three Managers Were Warned, Investigation Finds." Washington Post. www.washingtonpost.com/charlie-roses-misconduct-was-widespread-at-cbs-and-three-managers-were-warned-investigation-finds/2018/05/02/80613d24-3228-11e8-94fa-32d48460b955_story.html (accessed on October 08, 2021).

Broom, G.M. and B.-L. Sha. 2013. *Cutlip & Center's Effective Public Relations* (11th ed.).

Broom, G.M. and D.M. Dozier. 1986. "Advancement for Public Relations Role Models." *Public Relations Review* 12, pp. 37–56.

Brown, C.H. 1967. *The Correspondents' War: Journalists in the Spanish-American War*, p. 389. New York, NY: Schribner Publishing.

Brown, C. 2019. "Introducing Facebook News." Meta. https://about.fb.com/news/2019/10/introducing-facebook-news/ (accessed on October 08, 2021).

Browne, R. 2020. "Europe's Privacy Overhaul Has Led to $126 Million in Fines—But Regulators Are Just Getting Started." CNBC. www.cnbc.com/2020/01/19/eu-gdpr-privacy-law-led-to-over-100-million-in-fines.html (accessed on October 08, 2021).

Burns, E., N. Laskowski, and L. Tucci. n.d. "What Is Artificial Intelligence (AI)?" TechTarget. https://searchenterpriseai.techtarget.com/definition/AI-Artificial-Intelligence (accessed on October 08, 2021).

Burt, T. 2021. "7 Must-Have Public Relations Skills." https://muckrack.com/blog/2021/06/01/public-relations-skills (accessed on February 16, 2022).

Carvajal, E. n.d. "Arnold Schwarzenegger Confirmed That Maria Shiver Knew About His Affair for 'Many Years'." https://news.amomama.com/190268-arnold-schwarzenegger-confirmed-that-mar.html (accessed on October 08, 2021).

Cassidy, J. 2019. "Alex Acosta Had to Go, But the Jeffrey Epstein Scandal Is Really About Money and Privilege." New Yorker. www.newyorker.com/news/our-columnists/alex-acosta-had-to-resign-but-the-epstein-scandal-goes-well-beyond-his-role (accessed on August 20, 2021).

Center for an Informed Public. n.d. "About." University of Washington Center for an Informed Public. www.cip.uw.edu/about/ (accessed on October 08, 2021).

Chandran, M., L. DeFrancisco, S. Fugler, and E. Seasit. 2002. "Analyzing Credibility: A Study Examining Demographic Factors and Personality Traits That Influence Military Public Affairs' Credibility." DoD Joint Course in Communication, Class 02-A. University of Oklahoma. Accessed at www.ou.edu/deptcomm/dodjcc/groups/02A/index.htm.

Clabaugh, J. 2019. "The Washington Post Ends Publication of Express." WTOP News. https://wtop.com/business-finance/2019/09/the-washington-post-ends-publication-of-express/ (accessed on October 08, 2021).

Clarine, B. 2016. "1 Reasons Why Video Is Better Than Any Other Medium." www.advancedwebranking.com/blog/11-reasons-why-video-is-better/ (accessed on February 16, 2022).

Commission on Public Relations Education. 2017. "Fast Forward: The Commission on Public Relations Education 2017 Report on Undergraduate Education." www.commissionpred.org/commission-reports/fast-forward-foundations-future-state-educators-practitioners/ (accessed on February 16, 2022).

Corn, D. 2020. "Newly Released Transcripts Show Michael Flynn Betrayed the United States." Mother Jones. www.motherjones.com/politics/2020/05/newly-released-transcripts-show-michael-flynn-betrayed-the-united-states/ (access on October 08, 2021).

David M., D.K. Wright, and D.W. Stacks. n.d. "Evaluating Efficacy in Public Relations/Corporate Communication Planning: Towards Establishing Standards of Campaign Performance." *Public Relations Journal* 6, pp. 1–25.

Davies, W. 2019. "Why Can't We Agree on What's True Anymore?" The Guardian. www.theguardian.com/media/2019/sep/19/why-cant-we-agree-on-whats-true-anymore (accessed on October 08, 2021).

Defense Information School. n.d.a. "DINFOS History." www.dinfos.dma.mil/About/DINFOS-History/ (accessed on August 15, 2021).

Defense Information School. n.d.b. "PACS-Q." www.dinfos.dma.mil/Academics/DINFOS-Course-Catalog/DINFOS_PACS-Q/ (accessed on August 15, 2021).

Defense Information School. n.d.c. "Joint Intermediate Public Affairs Course Training Program of Instruction." www.dinfos.dma.mil/Portals/66/UPDATED_TPI_JIPAC_5_20_2020.pdf (accessed on August 15, 2021).

Defense Information School. n.d.d. "Information for Combat Camera Leadership Course (CCLC)." www.dinfos.dma.mil/Portals/66/Documents/Academics/PALD/CCLC.pdf (accessed on August 15, 2021).

Defense Information School. n.d.e. "Visual Information Management Course." www.dinfos.dma.mil/Portals/66/Documents/Academics/PALD/VIM.pdf (accessed on August 15, 2021).

Defense Information School. n.d.f. "Joint Contingency Public Affairs Course Training Program of Instruction." www.dinfos.dma.mil/Portals/66/SIGNED-JCPAC_TPI%2022%20May%202020_1.pdf (accessed on August 15, 2021).

Defense Information School. n.d.g. "Mass Communications Foundatiopns Course." www.dinfos.dma.mil/Academics/DINFOS-Course-Catalog/DINFOS_MCF/ (accessed on August 15, 2021).

Defense Information School. n.d.h. "About Pavilion." https://pavilion.dinfos.edu/About/ (accessed on August 15, 2021).

Dennis, E. 1992. *Of Media and People*, p. 10. Newbury Park: Sage Publications.

Department of Defense. 1993. *Joint Ethics Regulation*. DoD Instruction 5500.7-R. Washington, D.C.: Department of Defense. www.esd.whs.mil/Portals/54/Documents/DD/issuances/dodm/550007r.pdf.

Department of Defense. 2007. *Standards of Conduct*. DoD Directive 5500. Washington, D.C.: Department of Defense. www.esd.whs.mil/Portals/54/Documents/DD/issuances/dodd/550007p.pdf.

Department of Defense. 2012. Joint Publication 3-13, Information Operations. Washington, D.C.: Department of Defense. http://dtic.mil/doctrine/new_pubs/jp3_13.pdf.

Department of Defense. 2014. *Procedures for Joint Public Affairs Operations*. DoD Instruction 5400.14. Washington, D.C.: Department of Defense. www.esd.whs.mil/Portals/54/Documents/DD/issuances/dodi/540014p.pdf.

Department of Defense. 2016. Joint Publication 3-61, Public Affairs. Washington, D.C." Department of Defense. www.jcs.mil/Portals/36/Documents/Doctrine/pubs/jp3_61.pdf.

Department of Defense. 2017. *Assistant to the Secretary of Defense for Public Affairs (ATSD(PA))*. DoD Directive 5122.05. Washington, D.C.: Department of Defense. www.esd.whs.mil/Portals/54/Documents/DD/issuances/dodd/512205_dodd_2017.pdf?ver=2017-08-07-125832-023.

Department of the Air Force. 2018. "AFSC 35P Public Affairs Officer / Civilian Career Field Education And Training Plan." https://static.e-publishing.af.mil/production/1/saf_pa/publication/cfetp35p/cfetp35p.pdf (accessed on November 29, 2021).

Department of the Army. DA PAM 600–3. February 01, 2010. Washington, D.C.: Department of the Army. www.career-satisfaction.army.mil/resources/pdfs/DA%20Pamphlet%206003_Commissioned_Officer_Professional_Development_and_Career_Management.pdf.

Department of the Army. n.d. "Army Public Affairs: Telling the Army's Storey." www.army.mil/publicaffairs/ (accessed on August 15, 2021).

Dietrich, G. 2022. "Is 2022 the Year You (Finally) Embrace the PESO Model™?" https://spinsucks.com/communication/pr-pros-must-embrace-the-peso-model/ (accessed on February 16, 2022).

Dolphin, R. 2005. "Internal Communications: Today's Strategic Imperative." *Journal of Marketing Communications* 11, no.3, pp. 171–190.

Douglas, P. 2002. "No Bad Stories: The American Media-Military Relationship." *Naval War College Review* Vol. LV, no. 1, p. 87, Winter.

Edelman. 2018. "Edelman Trust Barometer." www.edelman.com/research/2018-delman-trust-barometer (accessed on October 08, 2021).

Edelman. 2020. "2020 Edelman Trust Barometer spring update: Trust and the Coronavirus." www.edelman.com/research/trust-2020-spring-update (accessed on October 08, 2021).

Edelman. n.d. "What Brands Need to Know About Covid-19 & Being Black in America." Insights & Implications. www.edelman.com/sites/g/files/aatuss191/files/2020-06/COVID-19%20and%20Being%20Black%20in%20America.pdf (accessed on October 08, 2021).

FBI. 2017. "Safe Online Surfing Internet Challenge." FBI. www.fbi.gov/news/stories/new-safe-online-surfing-internet-challenge (accessed on October 08, 2021).

Fox, E.J. 2017. "Brian Williams Opens Up About His Unexpected Re-Invention: 'Second Acts Are Possible, With A Little Spiffing Up.'" Vanity Fair. www.vanityfair.com/news/2017/10/brian-williams-11th-hour (accessed on October 10, 2021).

Gallup. Inc. n.d. "Confidence in Institutions." https://news.gallup.com/poll/1597/confidence-institutions.aspx (accessed October 08, 2021).

GDPR.EU. n.d. "Complete Guide to GDPR Compliance." GDPR.EU. https://gdpr.eu/ (accessed on October 08, 2021).

Grantham, R., Maj. USAFR. 2000. "Air War Over Serbia: It Is Important To Win The Information War." Alabama: Air Command and Staff College, Air University, Maxwell Air Force Base.

Greenhut, S. 2013. "Jounalism Is an Act, Not a Profession." Reason. https://reason.com/2013/07/12/journalism-is-an-act-not-a-profession/ (accessed on October 08, 2021).

Handke, L., E. Schulte, K. Schneider, and S. Kauffeld. 2018. "The Medium Isn't the Message: Introducing a Measure of Adaptive Virtual Communication." *Cogent Arts & Humanities* Vol. 5, Issue 1.

Headquarters Marine Corps. n.d. Communications Directorate. Washington, D.C.: U.S. Marine Corps. www.hqmc.marines.mil/ousmcc/.

Heshmat, S. 2015. "What Is Confirmation Bias?" Psychology Today. www .psychologytoday.com/us/blog/science-choice/201504/what-is-confirmation-bias (accessed on October 08, 2021).

Hubbard, L. 2021. "Here's What Matt Lauer Is Doing Now." Town and Country Magazine. www.townandcountrymag.com/society/a15845582/what-matt-lauer-is-doing-now/ (accessed on October 08, 2021).

Jenkins, H. 2019. "What the Press Doesn't Know About Ukraine." *Wall Street Journal.* https://www.wsj.com/articles/what-the-press-doesnt-know-about-ukraine-11569620897 (accessed on October 08, 2021).

Jones, J. and C. Lloyd. "Larger Majority Says Racism Against Black People Widespread." Gallup. https://news.gallup.com/poll/352544/larger-majority-says-racism-against-black-people-widespread.aspx (accessed on October 08, 2021).

Josephson, M. 2005. "Preserving the Public Trust: The Five Principles of Public Service Ethics." United States: Unlimited Pub.

Jurkowitz, M., A. Mitchell, L. Santhanam, S. Adams, M. Anderson, and N. Vogt. 2013. "The Changing TV News Landscape." Pew Research Center www .journalism.org/2013/03/17/the-changing-tv-news-landscape/ (accessed on October 08, 2021).

Kazden, B. 2017. "What 'Breaking News" Really Means in Today's World." Huffington Post. www.huffpost.com/entry/what-breaking-news-means_b_1 2549374 (accessed on October 08, 2021).

Keefe, J., Y. Zhou and J. Merrill. 2021. "The Present and Potential of AI in Journalism." https://knightfoundation.org/articles/the-present-and-potential-of-ai-in-journalism/ (accessed on February 16, 2022).

Keily, T.J. 2022. "5 Massive PR Trends in 2022 Your Brand Should Be Dominating." www.meltwater.com/en/blog/pr-trends-your-brand-should-be-dominating (accessed on February 16, 2022).

Kirby, J.F. 2000. "Shaping Today's Battlefield: Public Affairs as an Operational Function." *Naval War College Essays 2000.*

Kjaer, A.L. n.d. "Speaker Ideas." https://speakerideas.com/speaker/anne-lise-kjaer/ (accessed on April 12, 2022).

Kroll, M.M. 2017. "Coast Guard Public Affairs Program History: The Search for Symmetry." San Diego: San Diego State University, Proquest Dissertations Publishing.

Kurtz, H. n.d. "Embedded in Controversy." www.washingtonpost.com/wp-dyn/ articles/A36362-2003mar27.html (accessed on November 09, 2021).

Lamay, C., M. FitzSimon, and J. Sahadi, ed. 1991. *The Media at War: The Press and the Persian Gulf Conflict*, p. 11. New York, NY: Gannett Foundation Media Center.

Larson, N., J.K. Mortenson, and R. Miller. 2020. "What Is 'Futures Literacy' and Why Is It Important?" https://medium.com/copenhagen-institute-for-futures-studies/what-is-futures-literacy-and-why-is-it-important-a27f24b983d8 (accessed on February 16, 2022).

Lehman, S. 2017. "Coast Guard Public Affairs Middle Management and the Excellence Study." Syracuse, NY: Syracuse University. https://surface.syr.edu/cgi/viewcontent.cgi?article=1183&context=thesis (accessed on November 29, 2021).

Library of Congress. n.d. "The Spanish-American War: The United States Becomes A World Power." www.loc.gov/classroom-materials/spanish-american-war-the-united-states-becomes-a-world-power/ (accessed on November 09, 2021).

Little, N. 2020. "Why Integrated Communications Is the Future of Public Relations." https://spinsucks.com/communication/integrated-communications-pr-future/ (accessed on February 16, 2022).

Ma, A. and B. Gilbert. 2019. "Facebook Understood How Dangerous the Trump-Linked Data Firm Cambridge Analytica Could Be Much Earlier Than It Previously Said. Here's Everything That's Happened Up Until Now." Insider. www.businessinsider.com/cambridge-analytica-a-guide-to-the-trump-linked-data-firm-that-harvested-50-million-facebook-profiles-2018-3 (accessed on October 08, 2021).

Maldanodo, M. 2020. "AI in PR: The Conversation Has Just Begun." https://instituteforpr.org/ai-in-pr-the-conversation-has-just-begun/ (accessed on February 16, 2022).

Marantz, A. 2019. "The Dark Side of Techno-Utopianism." The New Yorker. www.newyorker.com/magazine/2019/09/30/the-dark-side-of-techno-utopianism (accessed on October 08, 2021).

McCarthy, N. 2018. "Americas Most and Least Trusted Professions." Forbes. www.forbes.com/sites/niallmccarthy/2018/01/04/americas-most-and-least-trusted-professions-infographic/ (accessed on October 08, 2021).

McLennan, S. and J. Miles. "Opinion: A Once Unimaginable Scenario: No More Newspapers." Washington Post. www.washingtonpost.com/news/theworldpost/wp/2018/03/21/newspapers/ (accessed on October 08, 2021).

Michaelson, D. and D.W. Stacks. 2017. *A Professional and Practitioner's Guide to Public Relations Research, Measurement, and Evaluation*, 3rd ed. New York, NY: Business Expert Press.

Middlebury Libraries. 2021. "Internet News, Fact-Checking, & Critical Thinking." Middlebury Library Guides. https://middlebury.libguides.com/internet/fact-checking (accessed on October 08, 2021).

Mitchell, A., A. Grieco, and N. Sumida. n.d. "American's Favor Protecting Information Freedoms Over Government Steps to Restrict False News Online." Pew Research Center. www.journalism.org/2018/04/19/americans-favor-protecting-information-freedoms-over-government-steps-to-restrict-false-news-online/ (accessed on October 08, 2021).

Mock, J.R. 1941. *Censorship 1917*, p. 103. Princeton, NJ: Princeton University Press.

Moshin, M. 2021. "10 Facebook Statistics Every Marketer Should Know in 2021." Oberlo. www.oberlo.com/blog/facebook-statistics (accessed on October 08, 2021).

Mueller, R. 2019. "Report on the Investigation Into Russian Interference in the 2016 Presidential Election." U.S. Department of Justice. www.justice.gov/storage/report.pdf (accessed on October 08, 2021).

Nathanman, J., RADM, USN. September–October 1999. "Triumph in Kosovo: Naval Aviation Keys Allied Success." Naval Aviation News.

Naval Personnel Command. 2002. MILPERSMAN 1212-010. Millington, Tennessee: Department of the Navy. www.mynavyhr.navy.mil/Portals/55/Reference/MILPERSMAN/1000/1200Classification/1212-010.pdf?ver=ym0SgICUh1wMdlE3RdpZcw%3d%3d.

Navy Bureau of Personnel. 2019. Program Authorization 103—PAO Direct Commissioning Program. Millington, Tennessee: Department of the Navy. www.mynavyhr.navy.mil/Career-Management/Community-Management/Officer/Active-OCM/Restricted-Line/Public-Affairs-Officer/.

Navy Bureau of Personnel. 2021. August 2021. *Lateral Transfer and Redesignation Board Letter of Instruction*. Millington, Tennessee: Department of the Navy. www.mynavyhr.navy.mil/Portals/55/Boards/Administrative/Transfer Redesignation/Lateral_Transfer_LOI_2021-08_Aug.pdf?ver=Lv0ED 44S94npjlohla_ueA%3D%3D.

Navy Chief of Information. 2020. "PA Career Progression Brief." www.mynavyhr.navy.mil/Career-Management/Detailing/Officer/Pers-44-Staff-RL/Public-Affairs/ (accessed on November 29, 2021).

Neill, M.S. and M.E. Drumwright. 2012. "PR Professionals as Organizational Conscience." *Journal of Mass Media Ethics* 27, no. 4, pp. 220–234.

Nelson, H.L. 1967. *Freedom of the Press from Hamilton to the Warren Court*, pp. 229–230. Indianapolis: Bobbs-Merrill.

New York Times. n.d. "Roman Catholic Church Sex Abuse Cases." www.nytimes.com/topic/organization/roman-catholic-church-sex-abuse-cases (accessed on October 08, 2021).

Nieman Lab. n.d. "Predictions for Journalism 2020." Nieman Lab. www.niemanlab.org/collection/predictions-2020/ (accessed on October 08, 2021).

Noor, I. 2020. "Confirmation bias." Simply Psychology. www.simplypsychology.org/confirmation-bias.html (accessed on October 08, 2021).

O'Malley, A. 1920. *Keystones of Thought*. New York, NY: Devlin-Adair.

Ocalya, A. (@metaviv). October 08, 2018. "Believable: The Terrifyin Future of Fake News." Twitter, 10:27 a.m. https://twitter.com/metaviv/status/963188182861864960.

Panetta, K. 2019. "Trending: 15 Apps Parents Should Know About." 47ABC. www.wmdt.com/2019/08/trending-15-apps-parents-should-know-about (accessed on October 08, 2021).

Panja, T. 2019. "Russia Banned From Olympics and Global Sports for 4 Years Over Doping." New York times. www.nytimes.com/2019/12/09/sports/russia-doping-ban.html (accessed on October 08, 2021).

Parker, L. 2015. "The Anti-Vaccine Generation: How Movement Against Shots Got Its Start." National Geographic. www.nationalgeographic.com/news/2015/2/150206-measles-vaccine-disney-outbreak-polio-health-science-infocus/ (accessed on October 08, 2021).

Peterson, A. n.d. "The Big Deal About Big Data & PR." www.commpro.biz/the-big-deal-about-big-data-pr/ (accessed on February 16, 2022).

PRSA. 2021. "Detailed Knowledge, Skills and Abilities Tested on the Computer-based Examination for Accreditation in Public Relations." www.prsa.org/docs/default-source/accreditation-site/apr-ksas-tested.pdf (accessed on October 04, 2021).

PRSA. 2022. "Voices4Everyone." https://voices4everyone.prsa.org.

PRSA. n.d.a. "Silver Anvil Awards." www.prsa.org/conferences-and-awards/awards/silver-anvil-awards (accessed on June 19, 2021).

PRSA. n.d.b. "About Public Relations." www.prsa.org/about/all-about-pr (accessed on June 15, 2021).

PRSA. n.d.c. "PRSA Code of Ethics." www.prsa.org/about/prsa-code-of-ethics. (accessed on September 29, 2021).

Public Broadcast System. n.d. "World War II Propaganda." www.pbs.org/wgbh/americanexperience/features/goebbels-propaganda/ (accessed October 08, 2021).

Public Relations Society of America (PRSA). n.d. "APRM-FAQ." www.praccreditation.org (accessed on June 16, 2021).

Quell, M. 2020. "More Countries Pass 'Fake News' Laws in Pandemic Era." Courthouse News. www.courthousenews.com/more-countries-pass-fake-news-laws-in-pandemic-era/ (accessed on October 08, 2021).

Quick, J. and H. Larson. 2018. "The Vaccine-Autism Myth Started 20 Years Ago. Here's Why It Still Endures Today." Time. https://time.com/5175704/andrew-wakefield-vaccine-autism/ (accessed on October 08, 2021).

Ransom, J. 2020. "Harvey Weinstein's Stunning Downfall: 23 Years in Prison." New York Times. www.nytimes.com/2020/03/11/nyregion/harvey-weinstein-sentencing.html (accessed on August 20, 2021).

Rayome, A. 2019. "Apple's Tim Cook Files Supreme Court Brief to Support DACA." CNET. www.cnet.com/news/apples-tim-cook-files-supreme-court-brief-to-support-daca/ (accessed on October 08, 2021).

Rogan, J. 2013. "Exclusive: McChrystal Was Shocked by Controversy Over Rolling Stone Article." Foreign Policy. https://foreignpolicy.com/2013/01/04/exclusive-mcchrystal-was-shocked-by-controversy-over-rolling-stone-article/.

Rogers, C. 2019. "How Artificial Intelligence And Big Data Will Affect The Future Of PR." Accessed at https://instituteforpr.org/how-artificial-intelligence-and-big-data-will-affect-the-future-of-pr/ (accessed on February 16, 2022).

Rosen, G., K. Harbath, N. Gleicher, and R. Leathern. 2019. "Helping to Protect the 2020 U.S. Elections." Meta. https://about.fb.com/news/2019/10/update-on-election-integrity-efforts/?utm_source=axios&utm_medium=am&utm_campaign=11_25%EF%BB%BF&axios_adlink=1&stream=top (accessed on October 08, 2021).

San Diego State University. n.d. "PAO Program." https://jms.sdsu.edu/academics/pao_program (accessed on August 15, 2021).

Schudson, M. 2019. "The Fall, Rise, and Fall of Media Trust." *Columbia Journalism Review*, Winter. www.cjr.org/special_report/the-fall-rise-and-fall-of-media-trust.php (accessed October 08, 2021).

Seifert, K. 2020. "What really happened during Deflategate? Five years later, the NFL's 'scandal' aged poorly." ESPN. www.espn.com/nfl/story/_/id/28502507/what-really-happened-deflategate-five-years-later-nfl-scandal-aged-poorly (accessed on October 08, 2021).

Shane, L. 2019. "Survey: Public Confidence in the Military Is High, Especially Among Older Generations." Military Times. www.militarytimes.com/news/pentagon-congress/2019/07/22/survey-public-confidence-in-the-military-is-high-especially-among-older-generations/ (accessed October 08, 2021).

Shearer, E. and K.E. Matsa. 2018. "News Use Across Social Media Platforms 2018." Pew Research Center. www.journalism.org/2018/09/10/news-use-across-social-media-platforms-2018/ (accessed on October 08, 2021).

Simonite, T. 2020. "The Professors Who Call 'Bullshit' on Covid-19 Misinformation." Wired. www.wired.com/story/professors-call-bullshit-COVID-19-misinformation/ (accessed on October 08, 2021).

Sinek, S. 2015. Facebook. www.facebook.com/simonsinek/posts/great-leaders-have-a-vision-of-the-future-that-does-not-yet-exist-and-an-ability/10153082778351499/ (accessed on October 08, 2021).

Spector, J. 2020. "Behind the scenes: The Capitol chaos when Eliot Spitzer resigned 10 years ago." Democrat and Chronicle. www.democratandchronicle.com/story/news/politics/albany/2018/03/08/behind-scenes-capitol-chaos-when-eliot-spitzer-resigned-10-years-ago/404266002/ (accessed on October 08, 2021).

Stacks, D. and D. Michaelson. 2010. *A Practitioner's Guide to Public Relations Research, Measurement and Evaluation*. New York, NY: Business Expert Press.

Stacks, D.W. n.d. *Primer of Public Relations Research*, 3rd ed. New York, NY: Guilford.

Standsberry, K., J. Anderson, and L. Raine. "Experts Optimistic About the Next 50 Years of Digital Life." Pew Research Center. www.pewresearch.org/

internet/2019/10/28/experts-optimistic-about-the-next-50-years-of-digital-life/?utm_campaign=2019-11-06+Rundown&utm_medium=email&utm_source=Pew (accessed on October 08, 2021).

Stephen P., Rear Admiral, U.S. Navy (Ret.), former Navy Chief of Information, telephone interview with lead author, May 19, 2022.

Stephens, L. 1978. "The Professional Orientation of Military Public Affairs Officers." *Public Relations Quarterly* Vol. 23, Issue 4, p. 19, Winter.

Strandberg, J.M. and O. Vigsø. 2016. "Internal Crisis Communication." *Corporate Communications: An International Journal* 21, no. 1, pp. 89–102.

Tapper, J. 2016. "Book for First Time Details Emails, Allegations in Petraeus Scandal." CNN. www.cnn.com/2016/03/28/politics/jill-kelley-david-petraeus-john-allen/index.html (accessed on October 08, 2021).

Tech Republic Staff. 2020. " Facebook Data Privacy Scandal: A Cheat Sheet." Tech Republic. www.techrepublic.com/article/facebook-data-privacy-scandal-a-cheat-sheet/ (accessed on October 08, 2021).

The Media Insight Project. 2016. "A New Understanding: What Makes People Trust and Rely on News." American Press Institute. www.american pressinstitute.org/publications/reports/survey-research/trust-news/single-page/ (accessed on October 08, 2021).

The Media Insight Project. 2018. "What the Public Expects From the Press (and What Journalists Think)." American Press Institute. www .americanpressinstitute.org/publications/reports/survey-research/public-expects-from-press/ (accessed on October 08, 2021).

The Reporters Committee for Freedom of the Press. n.d. "America's War Coverage." www.rcfp.org/journals/the-news-media-and-the-law-fall-2001/americas-war-coverage/ (accessed on November 09, 2021).

The Young Turks, Inc. n.d. "TYT—The Home of Progessives." Apple app. https://apps.apple.com/us/app/tyt-home-of-progressives/id1319576607 (accessed on October 08, 2021).

Thunberg, G. 2019. *No One Is Too Small to Make a Difference.* London: Penguin.

Today's Military. n.d.a. "Public Affairs Officers." www.todaysmilitary.com/careers-benefits/careers/public-affairs-officers (accessed on June 15, 2021).

Today's Military. n.d.b. www.todaysmilitary.com/careers-benefits/careers/public-affairs-officers (accessed on June 15, 2021).

U.S. Army. n.d. "Army Public Affairs: Telling the Army Story." www.army.mil/publicaffairs/ (accessed on June 15, 2021).

U.S. Coast Guard [USCG]. 2021. *External Affairs Manual.* Washington, D.C.: U.S. Coast Guard. https://media.defense.gov/2021/Jul/06/2002756460/-1/-1/1/CIM_5700_13A%20EA%20MANUAL%202021.PDF.

U.S. Marine Corps. n.d. "Entertainment Media Liaison Office." www.hqmc .marines.mil/ousmcc/Units/emlo/ (accessed on November 29, 2021).

Ungarino, R. 2019. "Kylie Jenner's Tweet That Whacked Snap's Stock Was One Year Ago—and Shares Have Never Really Recovered." Business Insider. https://markets.businessinsider.com/news/stocks/snap-stock-price-kylie-jenner-snapchat-tweet-year-ago-2019-2-1027973126 (accessed on October 08, 2021).

Universal Accreditation Board. 2017. "Study Guide for the Examination for Accreditation in Public Relations + Military Communication." https://accreditation.prsa.org/MyAPR/Content/Apply/APR-M/APR-M.aspx (accessed on October 21, 2021).

Venable, B. January–February 2002. "The Army and the Media." *Military Review*, p. 67.

Waddington, S. 2018. "PESO Explained for Marketing and Public Relations." https://wadds.co.uk/blog/peso-for-marketing-and-pr (accessed on February 16, 2022).

Wall Street Journal Editorial Board. 2022. "Hilary Clinton Did It." *Wall Street Journal*. www.wsj.com/articles/hillary-clinton-did-it-robby-mook-michael-sussmann-donald-trump-russia-collusion-alfa-bank-11653084709?mod=Searchresults_pos4&page=1 (accessed on May 23, 2022).

Wallace, C. 2016. "Obama Did Not Block the Pledge." Factcheck.org. www.factcheck.org/2016/09/obama-did-not-ban-the-pledge/ (accessed on October 08, 2021).

Washington Headquarters Service. n.d. DoD Directives (updated February 15, 2022). Washington, D.C.: Executive Services Directorate. www.esd.whs.mil/Directives/issuances/dodd/.

Weiner, M. and S. Kochhar. 2016. "Irreversible: The Public Relations Big Data Revolution." Institute for Public Relations Measurement Commission. https://instituteforpr.org/irreversible-public-relations-big-data-revolution/ (accessed on February 16, 2022).

West, J. and C. Bergstrom. 2017. " 'Calling Bullshit' Makes an Impact at Schools Across the Country." University of Washington Information School. https://ischool.uw.edu/news/2017/10/calling-bullshit-makes-impact-schools-across-country (accessed on October 08, 2021).

Westerheide, F. 2020. "China—The First Artificial Intelligence Superpower." Forbes. www.forbes.com/sites/cognitiveworld/2020/01/14/china-artificial-intelligence-superpower/ (accessed on October 08, 2021).

"What is Public Affairs." n.d. Quorum. www.quorum.us/public-affairs-dictionary/public-affairs-definition/ (accessed on June 19, 2021).

White, J. and D.M. Dozier. 1992. "Public Relations and Management Decision Making." In J.E. Grunig (ed.), *Excellence in public relations and communications management*. Hillsdale, N.J: L. Erlbaum Assoc.

Wikipedia. n.d.a. "Public Affairs, Military." https://en.wikipedia.org/wiki/ Public_affairs_(military) (accessed on June 15, 2021).

Wikipedia. n.d.b. "COVID-19 pandemic." https://en.wikipedia.org/wiki/ COVID-19_pandemic.

Wikipedia. n.d.c. "The Young Turks." https://en.wikipedia.org/wiki/The_Young_ Turks (accessed on October 08, 2021).

Wikipedia. n.d.d. "Richard Stengel." https://en.wikipedia.org/wiki/Richard_ Stengel (accessed on October 08, 2021).

Wikipedia. n.d.e. "Media Literacy. https://en.wikipedia.org/wiki/Media_literacy (accessed on October 08, 2021).

Wiseman, J. 2015. "Rush to Pass 'Fake News' Laws During Covid-19 Intensifying Global Media Freedom Challenges." International Press institute. https://ipi .media/rush-to-pass-fake-news-laws-during-COVID-19-intensifying-global- media-freedom-challenges/ (accessed on October 08, 2021).

Wooden, J. and J. Carter. 2014. *Coach Wooden's Pyramid of Success Playbook*. Grand Rapids, MI: Revell.

Wright, R. 2004. *Assessment of the DoD Embedded Media Program*, p. S-1. Alexandria, Virginia: Institute For Defense Analyses .

Yaffa, J. 2020. "Is Russian Meddling as Dangerous as We Think?" The New Yorker. www.newyorker.com/magazine/2020/09/14/is-russian-meddling-as- dangerous-as-we-think (accessed on October 08, 2021).

About the Authors

Bob "Pritch" Pritchard, APR, Fellow PRSA, Captain, U.S. Navy (Retired)

A retired member of the public relations faculty in the Gaylord College of Journalism and Mass Communication at the University of Oklahoma, "Pritch" has more than 23 years of experience as a U.S. Navy public affairs officer and more than 20 years of experience as a public relations educator.

He received his Bachelor of Science degree in Business Administration from Phillips University and a Master of Arts in Public Relations from Ball State University. After graduating with his bachelor's degree, "Pritch" joined the Navy as a Naval Aviator flying the A7-E Corsair II. After being medically grounded, "Pritch" was designated as a public affairs (relations) specialist where he served the last 23 of his 27 years in the Navy.

He completed his naval career as the director of public relations for the United States European Command in Stuttgart, Germany, his third consecutive Unified Command public relations position. In the span of those three assignments, he managed all U.S. military public relations activity in 73 countries, territories, and possessions in the Pacific and 91 countries in Africa, Europe, and the Middle East and for the Nation's strategic forces. He was the first public relations officer assigned to the elite U.S. Navy SEALs.

His teaching and research expertise includes student leadership development, student-run firms, strategic public relations planning, crisis communications, and media relations. While actively teaching, he served as the faculty adviser for the Stewart Harral chapter of the Public Relations Student Society of America (PRSSA) at OU and for Lindsey + Asp, the nationally affiliated student-run advertising and public relations firm in Gaylord College.

He is a member of the PRSA College of Fellows, the 2013 PRSA Outstanding Educator, the 2011-2015 PRSSA National Faculty Adviser, and a past chair of the PRSA Educators Academy.

Mari K. Eder, Maj. Gen., USA (Ret.)

Mari K. Eder, retired U.S. Army Major General, is a renowned speaker and author, and a thought leader on strategic communication and leadership. General Eder has served as Director of Public Affairs at the George C. Marshall European Center for Security Studies and as an adjunct professor and lecturer in communications and public diplomacy at the NATO School and Sweden's International Training Command. She served in a number of senior positions in the Pentagon, on the Army Staff, as Deputy Chief of Public Affairs and Deputy Chief of the Army Reserve, and with DoD's Reserve Forces Policy Board. General Eder speaks and writes frequently on communication topics in universities and for international audiences and consults on communications issues.

General Eder is the author of *Leading the Narrative: The Case for Strategic Communication,* published by the Naval Institute Press. Her latest communications book, *American Cyberscape,* was released in November 2020. An inspirational book, *The Girls Who Stepped Out of Line: Stories of Courage, Sacrifice, and Grit—the Women of* WWII, was published in the summer of 2021. When not writing, lecturing, or traveling, she works with rescue groups and fosters rescue dogs.

Kim Marks Malone, APR, Fellow PRSA, Commander, U.S. Navy (Ret.)

Kim Marks Malone is an accredited PR professional, a retired Navy public affairs officer, a part-time PR consultant, and a full-time Public Relations professor and adviser for Meeman 901 Strategies, a student-run strategic communication firm at the University of Memphis.

Kim enlisted in the Navy in 1986 and was commissioned as a public affairs officer via Officer Candidate School in 1996. In her last Navy assignment, she commanded the Navy Office of Community Outreach, the only grassroots-level public affairs command in the Navy. She also managed issues on the Navy's National News Desk, led the public affairs team aboard the nuclear-powered aircraft carrier USS Nimitz (CVN-68), oversaw communication for Navy operations and programs, worked overseas, and with submarines. Kim retired from the Navy after 29+ years of service and settled in Memphis, Tenn.

When she's not teaching public relations, she's busy helping Memphis small businesses and nonprofits, engaging with their customers and telling their stories as an independent PR consultant. Her specialties include social media management, media relations, crisis communication, issues management, and organizational communication. Kim is also an executive PR consultant for VoxOptima, a woman and service-disabled veteran-owned communications, consulting, and media relations company with offices in Washington, DC, and Albuquerque, New Mexico, where she provides executive brand and media training services to clients including the U.S. Navy.

Kim is a member of the PRSA College of Fellows, serves on the executive board of the Memphis PRSA Chapter, and is the 2022 Chair of the PRSA Southeast District.

Matthew Kroll, Commander, U.S. Coast Guard

Matthew currently serves as the Chief of Media Relations and is the primary spokesperson for the U.S. Coast Guard. He has more than 17 years of operational and public relations experience in the military. Originally from Southern California, Matthew received a Bachelor of Arts degree in Communications Studies from Sonoma State University and a Master of Arts in Communications from San Diego State University.

He began his professional career as a radio broadcaster before enlisting in the Coast Guard. Shortly after joining, Matthew was selected for Officer Candidate School, received his "wings of gold," and flew the MH-65 "Dolphin" helicopter as aircraft commander and instructor pilot. He served as the unit public affairs officer at Air Station San Francisco and Air Station Atlantic city before being selected for the Coast Guard's public affairs advanced education program. Upon completion of his graduate degree, Matthew managed all external communications for the Eleventh Coast Guard District, which includes the states of California, Nevada, Arizona, and Utah, as well as all rescue and counter-narcotics operations in the international waters off Central and South America.

Specializing in crisis communications, he led public information teams for multiple national-level incidents including Hurricane Harvey in Texas, Hurricane Lane in Hawaii, and the Conception Dive Boat fire in California. An expert on Coast Guard public affairs history, Matthew researched and published multiple articles documenting the service's notable communicators and overall public relations program.

Matthew is a member of California Public Information Officials, holds a Public Information Officer (PIO) qualification for type-I incidents (highest level), and his staff was recently recognized as the Coast Guard's Public Affairs Office of the Year.

Katie Cousins, Maj., U.S Air Force (Veteran)

Katie Cousins is a public affairs professional and Air Force veteran. She served for 10 years as an Air Force public affairs officer leading active-duty public affairs units. Her Air Force experience includes serving as the Deputy Chief of Public Affairs at Travis Air Force Base, California, the Chief of Public Affairs at Altus AFB, Oklahoma, and the Commander of the Air Force Public Affairs Training Detachment at Fort Meade, Maryland. She also served as an Instructor of Public Affairs and Communication Strategy at DINFOS, where she was selected as the 2018 DINFOS Instructor of the Year. She holds a Bachelor of Science Degree in Foreign Area Studies from the U.S. Air Force Academy, and a master's degree in International Relations and Conflict Resolution from American Military University. She is a featured speaker on communication measurement and evaluation and is the creator of the Sight Model, a PR tool for analysis and evaluation of campaign performance. She currently serves as the Manager of Global Technology Communications at Nike, Inc., in Beaverton, Oregon.

Skye Martin, APR+M, Maj., USMC

A Marine Corps Communication Strategy and Operations officer, **Skye Martin** has a broad range of experience in the military public affairs field, including a combat deployment in Helmand province, Afghanistan, marketing, and advertising in support of USMC recruiting, teaching, and mentoring military officers as a Public Affairs and Communication Strategy instructor at Defense Information School, and now as a special assistant to the Chairman of the Joint Chiefs of Staff. She earned her Accreditation in Public Relations + Military in 2017 and was named San Diego State University's Outstanding Master of Arts Graduate in Mass

Communication and Media Studies in 2018. She was presented the 2018 Rear Admiral T. McCreary Junior Public Affairs Alumni Award for integrating research and strategic planning skills into her work at DINFOS and was selected as the 2019 DINFOS Instructor of the Year.

Index

Accreditation, 9–10
Accreditation in public relations and
    military communication
    (APR+M), 24
Active publics, 60
Acts of God, 74
Advocacy, 22
Air Force, 115–117
Air Force PAO Career Planning, 116,
    117
Army, 107–109
Artificial intelligence (AI), 32, 45, 129
Augmented reality (AR), 130
Aware publics, 60

B.A.S.I.C. communication objective
    measurement model, 57, 82
Big Data, 127–128
Black Lives Matter, 47
Boundary spanning, 4
Broadcast media, 68–69

Change, 48–51, 139–143
Coast Guard, 116, 118–119
Coast Guard public affairs, 116,
    118–119
Coast Guard typical public affairs
    office, 118–119
Combat Camera Leadership Course
    (CCLC), 101–102
Committee on Public Information
    (CPI), 4
Communication leadership, 96–97,
    101, 102
Communication planning, 58
Communication tactics, 70–71
    crisis communications, 72–73,
        76–77
    emergency communications,
        75–76

risk communications, 73–74
social media, 71–72
Community relations, 79–83
Competition, 23
Conflicts of Interest, 23
Corporate social responsibility (CSR),
    79
Crisis communications, 72–73,
    76–77
Culture of service, 80–81

Defense Information School
    (DINFOS), 4, 99–104
Combat Camera Leadership Course
    (CCLC), 101–102
core elements, 100
Joint Contingency Public Affairs
    Course (JCPAC), 102–103
Joint Intermediate Public Affairs
    Course (JIPAC), 101
online learning, 104
PAVILION, 104
Public Affairs and Communication
    Strategy Qualification Course
    (PACS-Q), 99–100
technical training, 103–104
Defense Media Activity (DMA), 137
Deferred Action for Childhood
    Arrivals (DACA) program, 47
Department of Defense (DOD), 122,
    139
directives, 19–21
Department of Defense (DOD)
    Principles of Information, 11,
    17, 18–19
Developmental research, 56
Digital media, 69
Direct commissioning process,
    109–110
Disclosure of Information, 23

Education, 45–46, 139
Education with Industry (EWI)
        Program, 105
Effective public relations, 95
Emergency communications, 75–76
Ethics, 17–24
Espionage Act, 9
Excellence pyramid, 60–61
Execution phase, 58
Expertise, 22–23
External information, 67–77

Facebook, 31
Fairness, 23
FBI Safe Online Surfing (FBI-SOS)
        program, 46
Free Flow of Information, 23

General Data Protection Regulation
        (GDPR), 31

Honesty, 22

Independence, 23
Information apocalypse, 27–35, 39,
        42, 49, 141
Information-based live events, 138
Information environment, 93–95
Information sources, 39–41
Information subsidies, 70
Institutional trust, 32
Internal information, 63–65
Internal stakeholders, 63–65
Intervening publics, 60

Joint Contingency Public Affairs
        Course (JCPAC), 102–103
Joint Intermediate Public Affairs
        Course (JIPAC), 101

Key publics, 59

Latent publics, 60
Lateral transfer, 110–111
Law of primacy, 67
Leadership, 60, 92, 95–97
Live events, 137–138

Loyalty, 23

Marine Corps, 111, 115
Marketing, 93
Mass Communication Foundations
        (MCF), 103
Media, 10–12
   in change, 48–49
   engagements, 70–71
   outlets, 68–69
   public affairs officer (PAO)
        responsibilities, 86–87
   public engagement with, 47
Media bias chart, 29–30
Media literacy, 42
Memorandum of understanding
        (MOU), 23
Michaelson and Macleod's best
        practices model, 56
Military–media relationship
   in World War I, 8–9
   in World War II, 9, 10
Military public affairs, 24, 63, 70,
        72, 83
   future trends, 127–143
   history, 7–15
   introduction to, 3–6
   personnel, 22
   vs. public relations, 91–93

Navy, 109–114
New media, 134–135
Nonpublics, 60

Operational mishaps, 74

PAVILION, 104
Personnel issues, 74
PESO Model, 134–136
Print media, 69
Proactive communications, 67
Professionalism, 17–24, 34, 37, 38,
        41
Professional values, 22–23
Profession enhancement, 23
PRSA Code of Ethics, 22
PRSA Code "Provisions of Conduct,"
        23

Public Affairs and Communication
    Strategy Qualification Course
    (PACS-Q), 99–100
Public affairs officer (PAO), 3, 17,
    33–34
  adviser, 95
  and change, 51
  communication leader, 96–97
  education, 99–106
  effective communicator, 91
  employment, 121–123
  formal education for, 132
  leadership, 95
  liaison, 95
  measurement and evaluation, 135
  military public affairs *vs.* public
    relations, 91–93
  qualifications and accession
    Air Force, 115–117
    Army, 107–109
    Coast Guard, 116, 118–119
    Marine Corps, 111, 115
    Navy, 109–114
  Research, Planning,
    Implementation, and
    Evaluation (RPIE) (*see*
    Research, Planning,
    Implementation, and
    Evaluation (RPIE))
  responsibilities, 85–88
  roles and responsibilities, 130–131
  spokesperson, 95
  training, 99–106
  upskilling, 132–134
Public affairs personnel, 3–4
Public information, 4

Qualifications and accession criteria,
    PAO
  Air Force, 115–117
  Army, 107–109
  Coast Guard, 116, 118–119
  Marine Corps, 111, 115
  Navy, 109–114
Qualitative research, 56

Reactive communications, 67
Research, Planning, Implementation,
    and Evaluation (RPIE), 4, 55,
    110
Responsibilities, PAO, 85–88
Risk communications, 73–74

Safeguarding Confidences, 23
Sedition Act, 9
Segmentation, 59, 60
Situation analysis (SA), 56–57, 128
Social activism, 47
Social media, 29, 33, 38, 49, 64, 69,
    71–72, 130, 140
Stakeholders, 58–59, 63–65
Strategic planning, 58, 60–61

Telegraph, 7–8
Transparent communications, 67
Trust, 32, 39–43
Two-way communication leadership,
    96–97

Virtual reality (VR), 130

Young Turks (TYT), 40

OTHER TITLES IN THE PUBLIC RELATIONS COLLECTION

Donald Wright, Boston University and Don Stacks, University of Miami, Editors

- *The Untold Power* by Melody Fisher
- *The PR Knowledge Book* by Sangeeta Waldron
- *An Overview of The Public Relations Function* by Shannon A. Bowen, Brad Rawlins, and Thomas R. Martin
- *Public Relations Ethics* by Marlene S. Neill and Amy Oliver Barnes
- *The New Era of the CCO* by Roger Bolton, Don W. Stacks, and Mizrachi Eliot
- *A Communication Guide for Investor Relations in an Age of Activism* by Marcia Distaso, David Michaelson, and John Gilfeather
- *Corporate Communication Crisis Leadership* by Ronald C. Arnett, Sarah M. Deluliis, and Matthew Corr
- *A Professional and Practitioner's Guide to Public Relations Research, Measurement, and Evaluation* by David Michaelson and Donald W. Stacks
- *Excellence in Internal Communication Management* by Rita Linjuan Men and Bowen Shannon

Concise and Applied Business Books

The Collection listed above is one of 30 business subject collections that Business Expert Press has grown to make BEP a premiere publisher of print and digital books. Our concise and applied books are for...

- Professionals and Practitioners
- Faculty who adopt our books for courses
- Librarians who know that BEP's Digital Libraries are a unique way to offer students ebooks to download, not restricted with any digital rights management
- Executive Training Course Leaders
- Business Seminar Organizers

Business Expert Press books are for anyone who needs to dig deeper on business ideas, goals, and solutions to everyday problems. Whether one print book, one ebook, or buying a digital library of 110 ebooks, we remain the affordable and smart way to be business smart. For more information, please visit www.businessexpertpress.com, or contact sales@businessexpertpress.com.